Scott Foresman - Addison Wesley
MATH

Enrichment Masters
Extend Your Thinking

Grade 1

Scott Foresman - Addison Wesley

Editorial Offices: Menlo Park, California • Glenview, Illinois
Sales Offices: Reading, Massachusetts • Atlanta, Georgia • Glenview, Illinois
Carrollton, Texas • Menlo Park, California

http://www.sf.aw.com

ISBN 0–201–31260–3

Printed in the United States of America

1 2 3 4 5 6 7 8 9 10 – BW – 02 01 00 99 98 97

Contents

Overview

Extend Your Thinking *(Enrichment Masters)* enhance student learning by actively involving students in different areas of mathematical reasoning. These masters consist of four types of motivating and challenging activities that focus on higher-order thinking skills. The categories are Patterns, Critical Thinking, Visual Thinking, and Decision Making.

Patterns activities encourage students to develop skills in recognizing patterns that exist in all facets of mathematics. The study of patterns allows students to gain an appreciation for the inter-relatedness and beauty in the structure of mathematics. These activities cover data, numbers, algebra and geometry, and allow students to find interesting solutions to sometimes difficult problems.

Critical Thinking activities challenge students to examine and evaluate their own thinking about math and about related content areas. The strategies students will use include: Classifying and Sorting, Ordering and Sequencing, Using Logic, Drawing Conclusions, Using Number Sense, Making Generalizations, Reasoning with Graphs and Charts, Explaining Reasoning/Justifying Answers, Developing Alternatives, Evaluating Evidence and Conclusions, and Making and Testing Predictions.

Visual Thinking activities focus on students' ability to perceive and mentally manipulate visual images. Emphasis is placed on spatial perception and visual patterns.

Decision Making activities present real-world situations that require students to make a decision. In most cases, there are no clearly right or wrong answers. This gives students the opportunity to carefully weigh alternate courses of action—as well as consider their personal experiences. You may wish to encourage students to use these decision-making steps as they make and evaluate their decisions:

Understand Encourage students to define the problem. They need to consider why a decision is needed, what goal they wish to meet, and what tools and techniques they can use to reach their decision.

Plan and Solve Have students identify the information that is relevant to the decision-making process.

Make a Decision After students evaluate the data and consider the consequences, they decide which choice is best.

Present the Decision Students explain why they made the choice that they did.

Name _____

Patterns in Geometry

Look at the pattern in each row.
Draw what comes next.

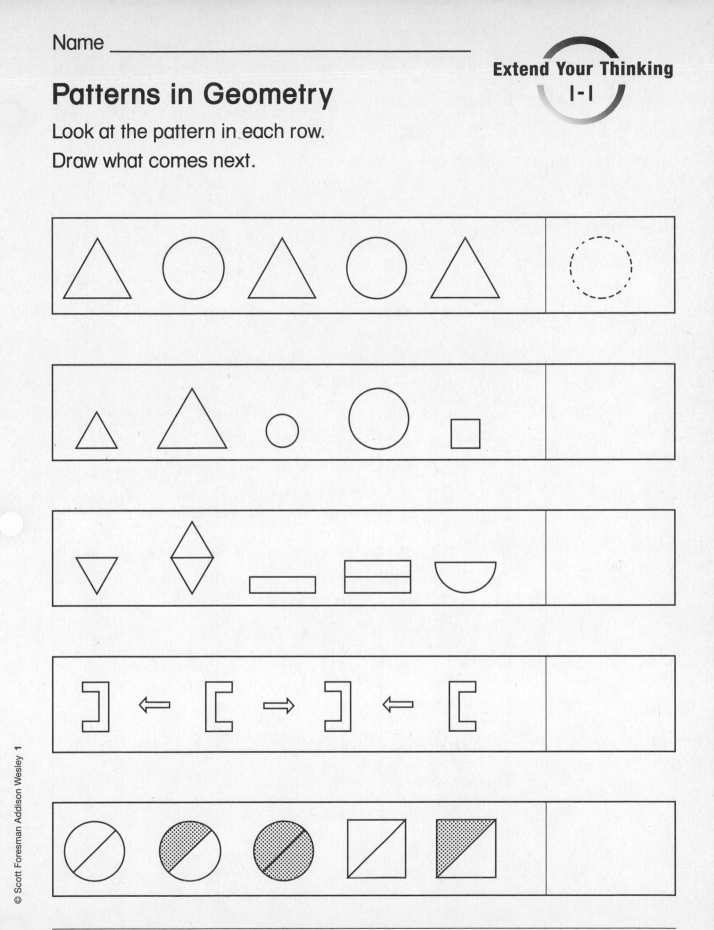

Notes for Home Your child completed a pattern in each row by drawing the shape that came next in the pattern.
Home Activity: Ask your child to explain one of the patterns to you.

Name _____

Critical Thinking

Four animals walked on the sand.

Draw lines to match each animal with its track.

Notes for Home Your child used visual clues to identify which animal made each trail, and drew lines to connect the animal's picture with its footprints. *Home Activity:* Ask your child to explain his or her reasoning.

Name _____

Visual Thinking

Look at these shapes.

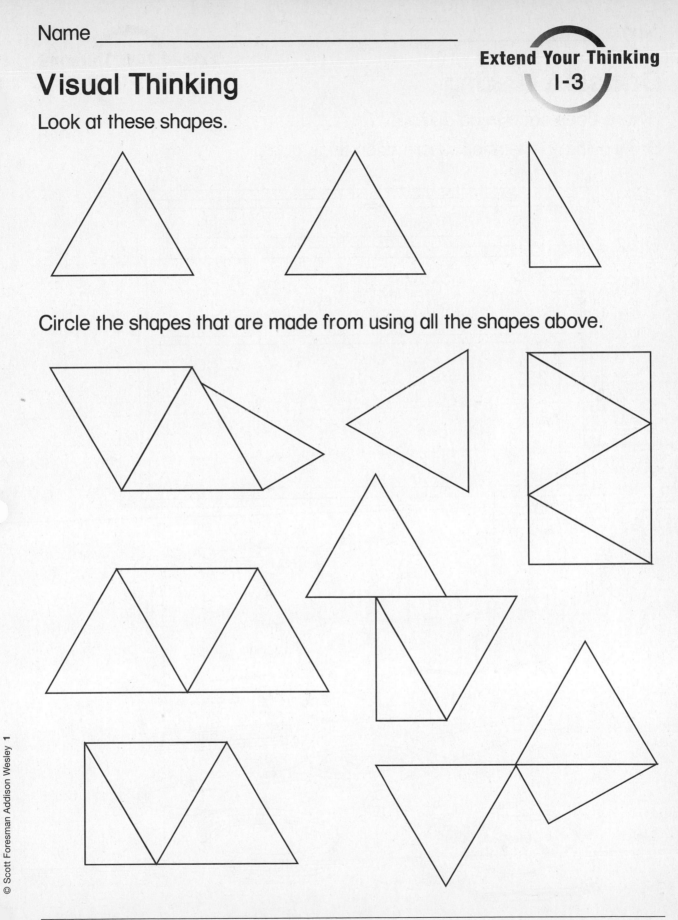

Circle the shapes that are made from using all the shapes above.

Notes for Home Your child matched objects of the same shape and number by circling the figures that used the given shapes. *Home Activity:* Have your child cut out the shapes in the top row and use them to make the figures they circled. Encourage your child to create additional figures.

Name _____

Decision Making

Where does each thing go?

Draw a line to the shelf where each thing goes.

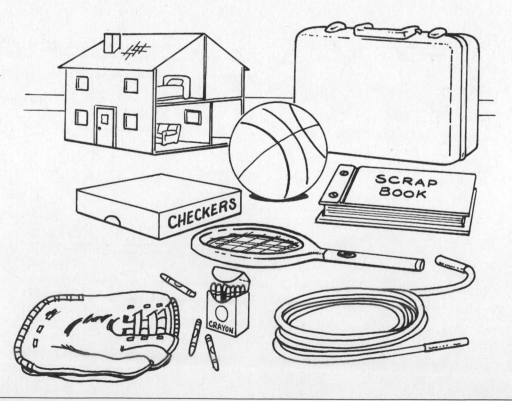

CHECKERS

SCRAP BOOK

CRAYON

Notes for Home Your child considered how big and heavy each object is before deciding where it should be stored. *Home Activity:* Ask your child to choose a good place in your home for each of the pictured objects and then explain his or her choices.

Name _____

Visual Thinking

Count how many are in each group.

Draw lines to match the groups.

© Scott Foresman Addison Wesley 1

Notes for Home Your child counted and compared the number of objects in groups. *Home Activity:* Assemble a group of at least 20 small objects such as paper clips or spoons. Separate out a group of up to 10 objects and ask your child to make a matching group with the same number of objects in it. Then reverse roles.

Critical Thinking

Look for clues in each picture.
Then write the number.

How many cats are there? _____

How many horses are there? _____

How many people are there? _____

How many skaters are there? _____

Notes for Home Your child looked at a picture and used clues to draw conclusions. *Home Activity:* Ask your child to explain his or her reasoning for each answer.

6 Use with pages 15–16.

Name _____

Critical Thinking

Circle the boxes that are just right for the foods.

Draw an X on each wrong box.

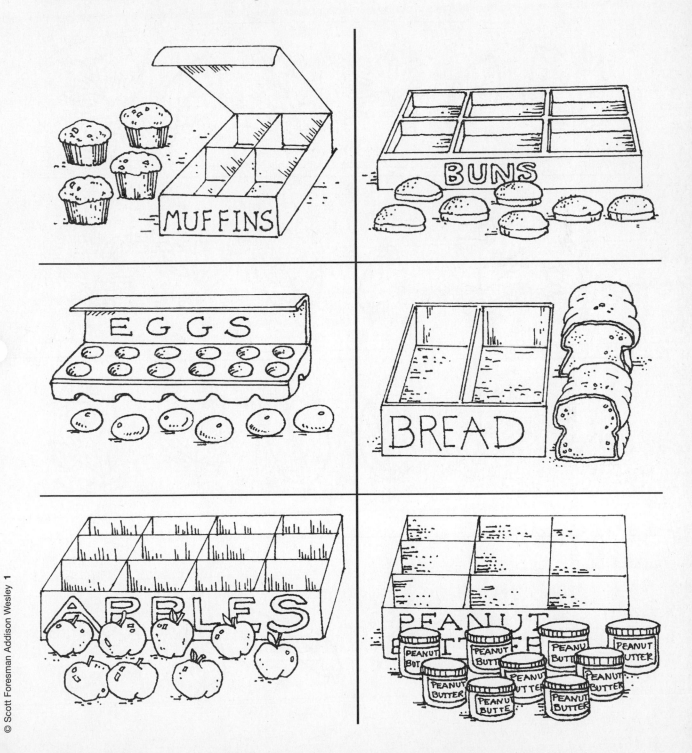

© Scott Foresman Addison Wesley 1

Notes for Home Your child crossed out each box that had more or fewer compartments than the number of objects to be placed in it. *Home Activity:* Ask your child to compare two groups of objects—such as socks and shirts in a drawer, or peas and French fries on a plate—and identify which group has more and which has less.

Patterns in Geometry

Circle each row that shows a pattern.

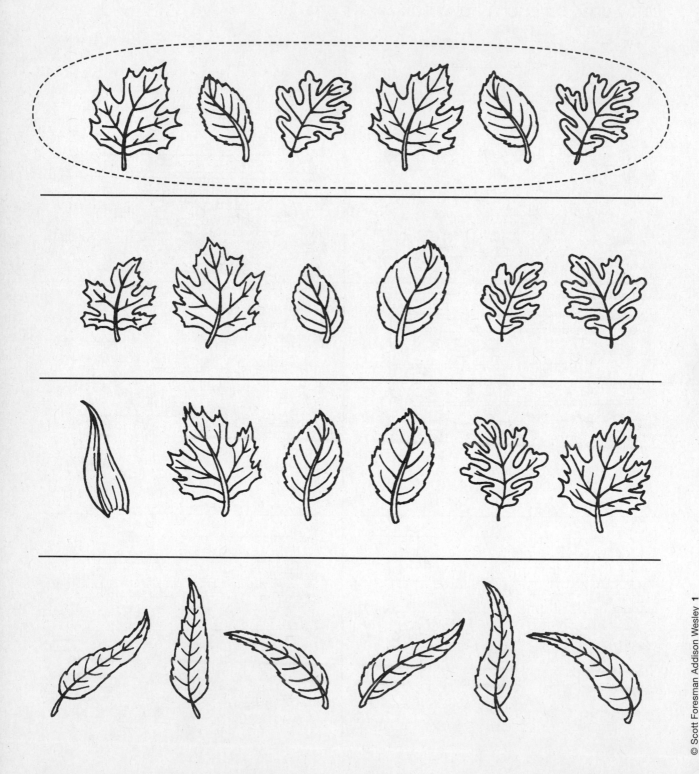

© Scott Foresman Addison Wesley 1

Notes for Home Your child decided whether each row of leaves followed a pattern. *Home Activity:* Ask your child to draw the leaf that would come next in each row that shows a pattern.

Name _____

Decision Making

Which teams played each other?

Match each winning team with a losing team.

Draw a line.

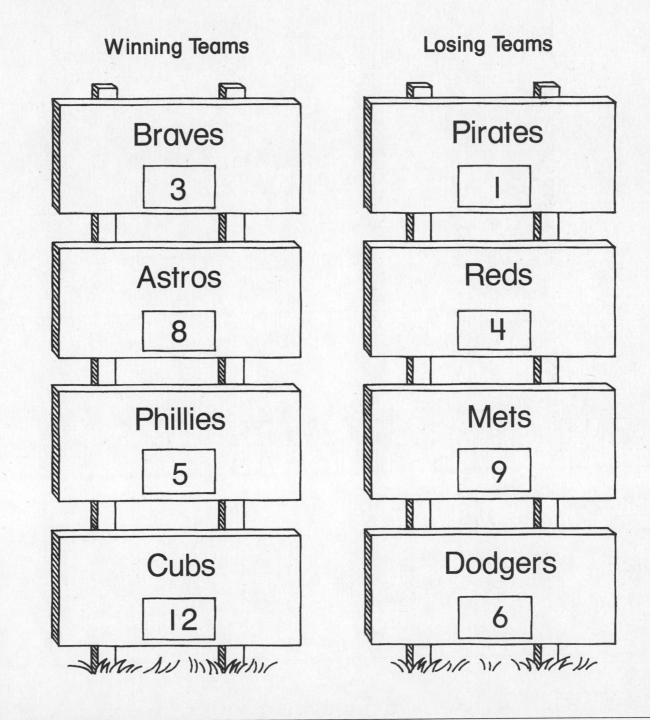

Winning Teams	Losing Teams

Braves 3

Astros 8

Phillies 5

Cubs 12

Pirates 1

Reds 4

Mets 9

Dodgers 6

© Scott Foresman Addison Wesley 1

Notes for Home Your child decided which teams played each other based on winning and losing scores.
Home Activity: Ask your child to explain his or her choices.

Name _____

Patterns in Numbers

Read each row.

Draw and write what comes next.

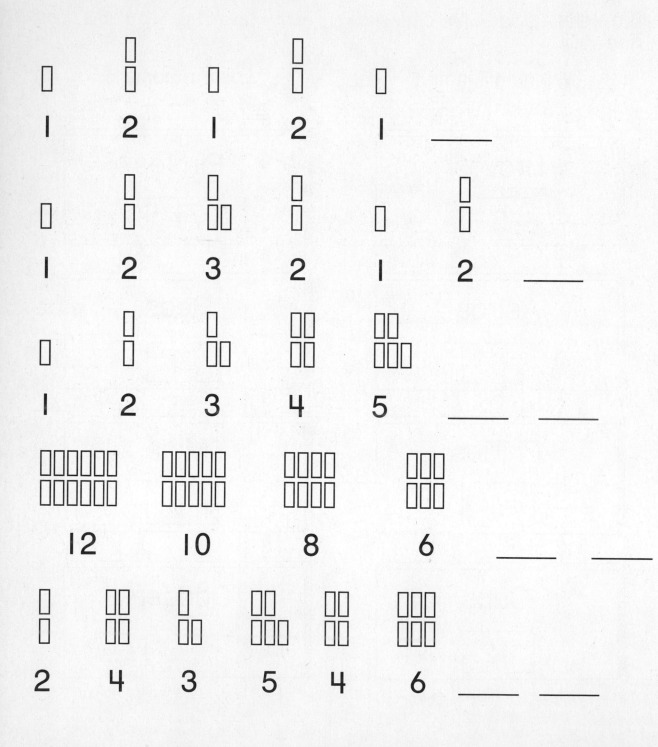

1   2   1   2   1   ___

1   2   3   2   1   2   ___

1   2   3   4   5   ___   ___

12   10   8   6   ___   ___

2   4   3   5   4   6   ___   ___

Notes for Home Your child identified the next number in a pattern involving numbers up to 12. *Home Activity:* Have your child use index cards or sports cards to show the patterns above and then to make up original patterns with numbers.

Name _____

Decision Making

These children need some help.
Circle the item each child could use.

© Scott Foresman Addison Wesley 1

Notes for Home Your child circled the object that was most appropriate in solving each of three problems.
Home Activity: Ask your child to explain each pictured problem and the reason for his or her choice.

Visual Thinking

The key opens doors that show two things.

How will the girl get out?

Draw a line.

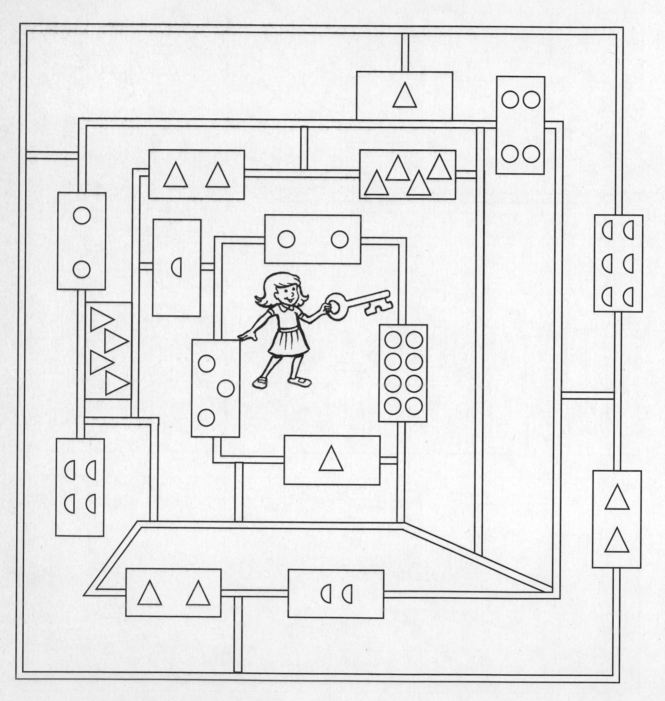

© Scott Foresman Addison Wesley 1

Notes for Home Your child identified the correct path through a maze by drawing a line from the center to the exit.
Home Activity: Ask your child to find things around the house that come in twos, such as shoes, mittens, and salt and pepper shakers.

Name _____

Critical Thinking

A class voted for the best season.

Look at the graph.

Answer the questions.

How many like ☀ best? _____

How many like 🍃 best? _____

How many like ❄ best? _____

How many like ☂ best? _____

Which season got the most votes? _____

Notes for Home Your child read a picture graph showing opinions on the best of the four seasons and answered questions about it. *Home Activity:* Ask your child to conduct a survey of your family to see which season each member likes best. Help your child draw a picture graph similar to this one, using his or her findings.

Name _____

Decision Making

You win 12 [**Ticket**] at the fair.

Circle the prizes you would choose.

© Scott Foresman Addison Wesley 1

Notes for Home Your child decided which prizes he or she would choose with a value of up to 12. *Home Activity:* Ask your child to identify the most expensive prize (teddy bear) and the least expensive prize (gum).

14 Use with pages 37–38.

Name _____

Decision Making

The number on each car tells you
how many clowns will fit in it.
For each car, circle the two groups that will fill it up.

Notes for Home Your child identified various ways to show the numbers 4 and 5. *Home Activity:* Find a set of five small objects, such as pencils. Ask your child to show you three ways he or she can arrange the five pencils in two groups. Do the same for four objects.

Visual Thinking

Balance the scales.
Draw what is missing.

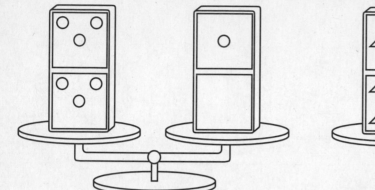
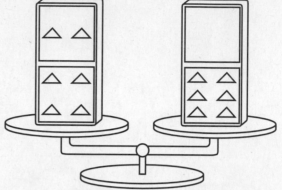

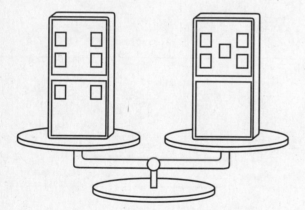
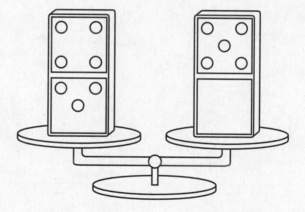

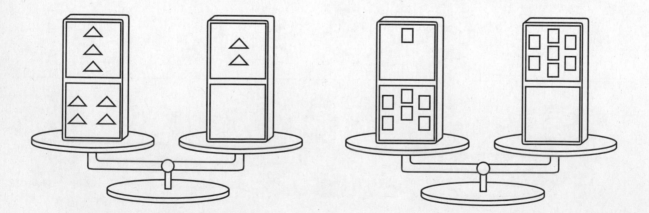

Notes for Home Your child drew what was missing to show the number 6 or 7. *Home Activity:* Ask your child to show you all the ways to arrange seven cans in two groups.

Critical Thinking

Circle each shape with only 8 parts.

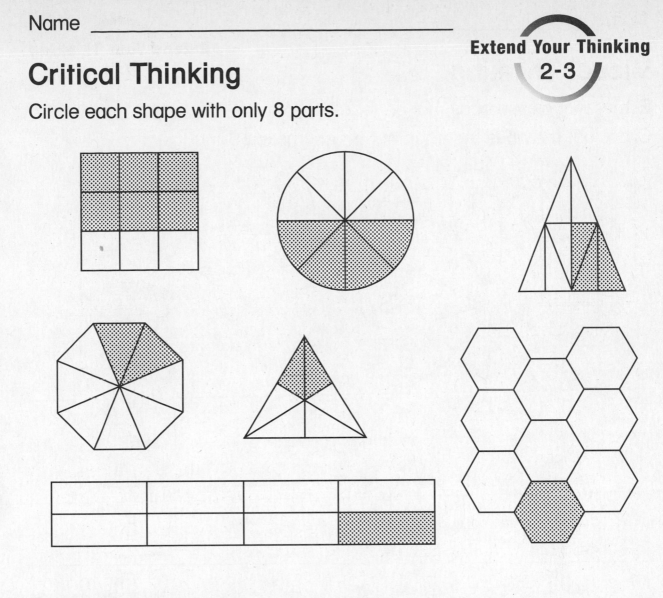

Which shapes below use only shaded parts from
the shapes circled above?
Color those shapes. Cross out the others.

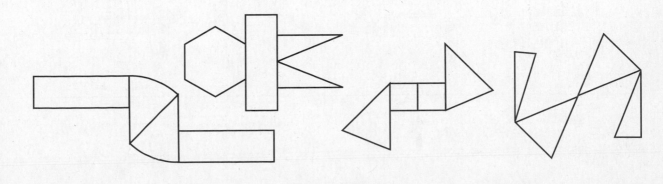

Notes for Home First your child circled the shapes with only eight parts. Then he or she colored designs made of
parts matching those in the circled shapes. *Home Activity:* Fold and cut a piece of paper into eight parts. Ask your
child to show all the ways that two people could share the eight parts.

Name _____

Visual Thinking

Each row has two cans that go together to make 10.
Cross out the ones that together do not make 10.

Notes for Home Your child identified two numbers in each row that equal 10 and then crossed out two numbers that do not equal ten. *Home Activity:* Ask your child to name three sets of numbers that equal 10, such as 6 + 4, 7 + 3, and 8 + 2.

© Scott Foresman Addison Wesley **1**

Patterns in Geometry

See how the shape turns.

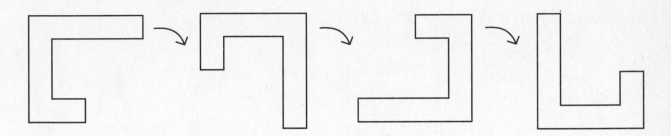

How will each shape turn next? Circle the correct one.

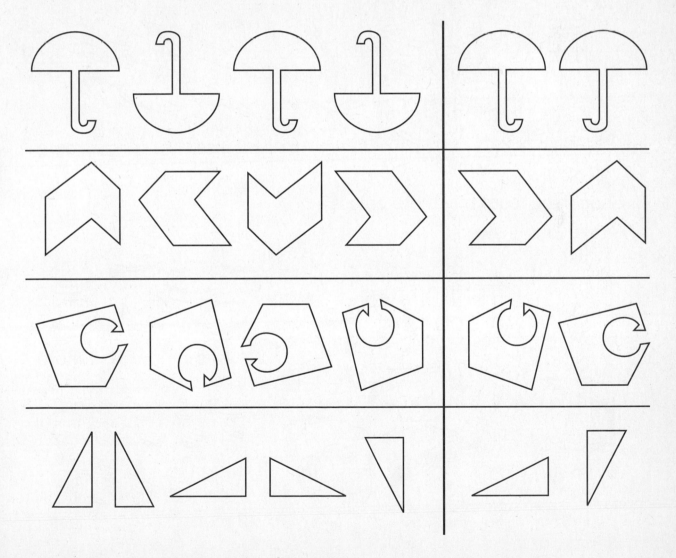

Notes for Home Your child circled the shape that showed the next position of the shape in each row.
Home Activity: Ask your child to explain one of the rows to you.

Name _____

Decision Making

Each person gets 1 thing.

1. Should Mom buy more or less?
   Circle your answers.

1 more   1 less

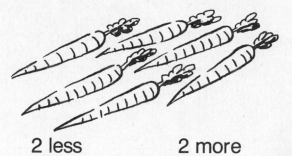

2 less   2 more

2. Should the team buy more or less?
   Circle your answers.

1 less   2 more

2 more   1 less

Notes for Home Your child used picture clues to buy 1 or 2 more, or 1 or 2 less items. *Home Activity:* Ask your child to tell the number that is 1 more than the number of members in your family, and to tell the number that is 2 less than the number of members in your family.

Name _____

Visual Thinking

Find the boxes with odd numbers. Color them red.

Find the boxes with even numbers. Color them blue.

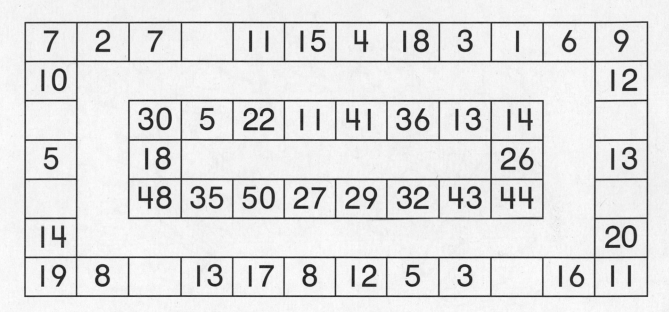

7	2	7		11	15	4	18	3	1	6	9
10											12
		30	5	22	11	41	36	13	14		
5		18						26			13
		48	35	50	27	29	32	43	44		
14											20
19	8		13	17	8	12	5	3		16	11

Color the boxes with odd numbers orange.

Color the boxes with even numbers yellow.

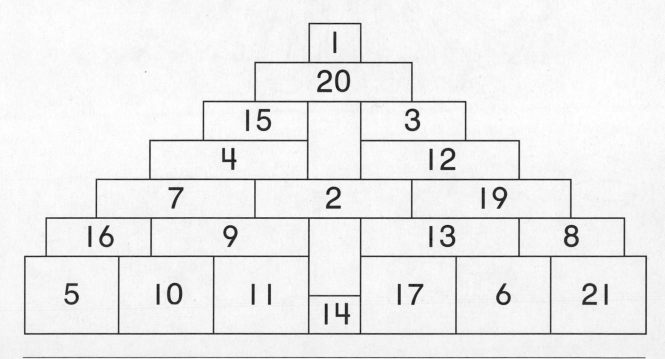

Notes for Home Your child identified numbers as odd or even. *Home Activity:* Ask your child to count to 19 by odds; count to 20 by evens.

Critical Thinking

The 12 Monster needs 12 of everything.

Circle how many more of each thing it needs.

Notes for Home Your child matched items needed to complete sets of 12. *Home Activity:* Ask your child: *If the 12 monster has 6 boots, how many more does it need?* (6) *If the 12 monster has 7 whistles, how many more does it need?* (5)

22 Use with pages 69–70.

Decision Making

Help the children pack for a trip.

Dan has room for 6 things. He has 2.
What other things can he take?
Circle the things in red.

Pat has room for 4 things. She has 1.
What other things can she take?
Circle the things in blue.

Bob has room for 7 things. He has 6.
What other things can he take?
Circle the things in green.

Notes for Home Your child decided how many and what kinds of items to take on a trip after being told how many could fit into a suitcase. *Home Activity:* Ask your child to explain his or her choices.

Patterns in Numbers

In each row, draw more O to make 10 in all.
Write how many O you draw in each row.
Color all the O you draw with the same color.

A   **B**

1 | O | _____

2 | O O | _____

3 | O O O | _____

4 | O O O O | _____

5 | O O O O O | _____

6 | O O O O O O | _____

7 | O O O O O O O | _____

8 | O O O O O O O O | _____

9 | O O O O O O O O O | _____

Draw a line from each sentence to its ending.

1. In column A, the numbers

2. In column B, the numbers

get 1 smaller.

get 1 bigger.

stay the same.

Notes for Home Your child drew circles to complete sets of ten, compared amounts, and identified a pattern on a chart. *Home Activity:* Ask your child to find two lines that use the numbers 7 and 3, and tell how their pictures are alike and different.

Name _____

Critical Thinking

Each dog had 7 bones.

Each dog lost some.

How many does each dog have left?

Write the number.

	Lost on Day 1	Lost on Day 2	How many are left?
			_____
			_____
			_____
			_____

Circle the answer.

1. Who has more bones now?

2. Who lost more bones?

3. Who lost the most bones?

4. Who took the best care of the bones?

Notes for Home Your child read a chart and answered questions about it. *Home Activity:* Ask your child which dog has the most bones now (the smallest dog) and which dog has the least (the dog with spots).

© Scott Foresman Addison Wesley 1

Name _____

Visual Thinking

Find all the ⟨mitten⟩ hidden in the picture.

Color them red.

Find all the ⟨sled⟩ hidden in the picture.

Color them green.

Finish these sentences.

I found _____ ⟨mitten⟩ and _____ ⟨sled⟩ .

I colored _____ things.

© Scott Foresman Addison Wesley 1

Notes for Home Your child found and colored things hidden in a picture and then totaled the number of objects that were colored. *Home Activity:* Hide objects such as 4 mittens and 3 shoes in the living room or kitchen. Have your child find them, bring them to you, and tell how many objects were found in all.

Critical Thinking

These pictures show four turns in a game of jacks.

Match 2 number sentences with each picture.

Complete each number sentence.

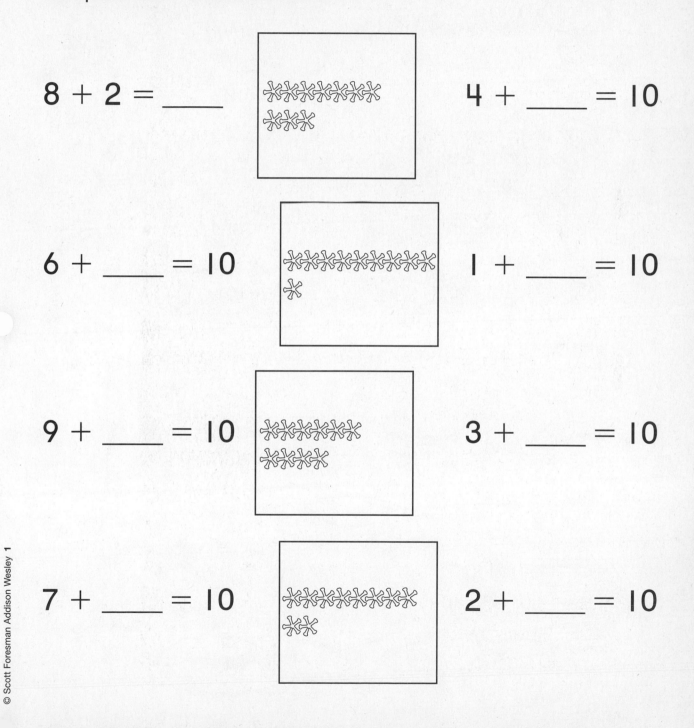

$8 + 2 =$ ___

$4 +$ ___ $= 10$

$6 +$ ___ $= 10$

$1 +$ ___ $= 10$

$9 +$ ___ $= 10$

$3 +$ ___ $= 10$

$7 +$ ___ $= 10$

$2 +$ ___ $= 10$

Notes for Home Your child identified two addition sentences that describe each picture. *Home Activity:* Show several fingers on one hand and a different number of fingers on the other. Ask your child to state two addition sentences that describe the groups of fingers you are showing.

Name ______________________________

Extend Your Thinking 3-3

Decision Making

Find the sums.

Draw lines to match the animals with their homes.

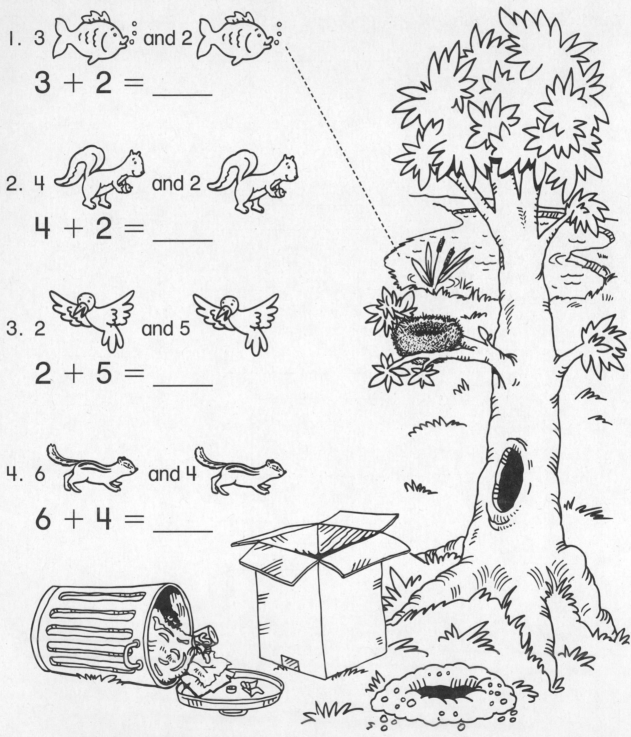

1. 3  and 2 

$3 + 2 =$ ____

2. 4  and 2 

$4 + 2 =$ ____

3. 2  and 5 

$2 + 5 =$ ____

4. 6  and 4 

$6 + 4 =$ ____

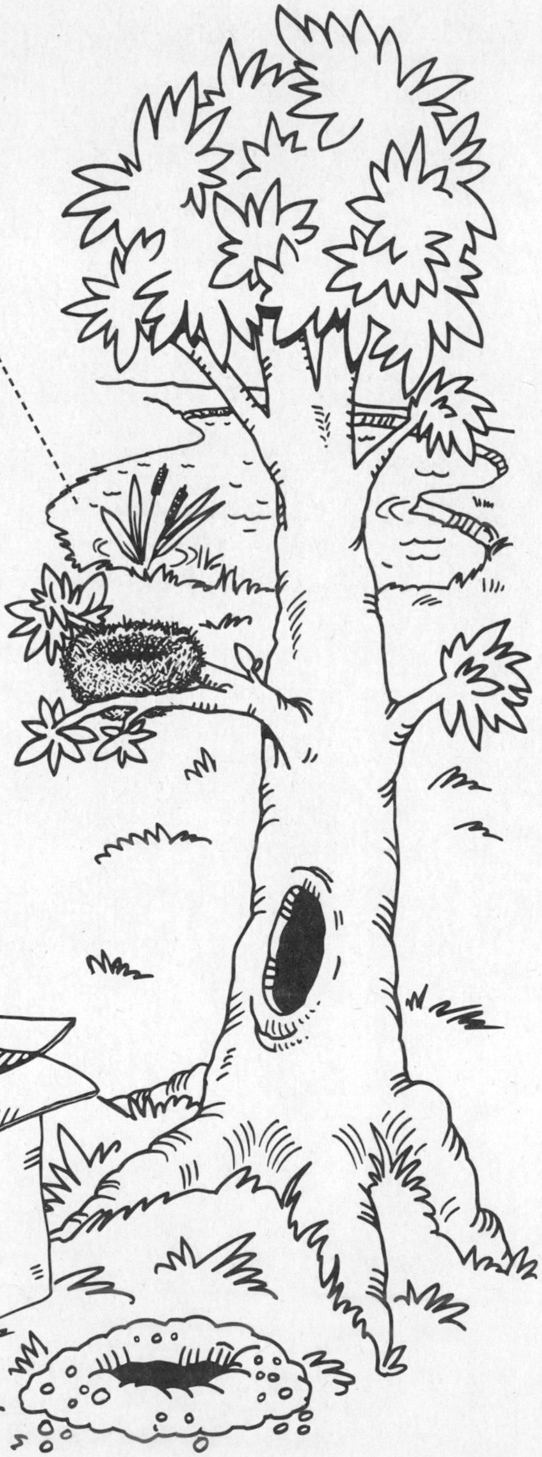

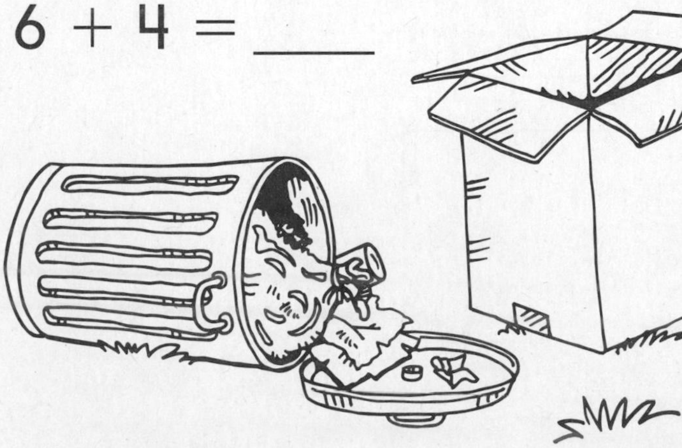

Notes for Home Your child completed addition sentences and then chose homes for animals. *Home Activity:* Ask your child to explain his or her choices of animal homes.

Name ______________________

Extend Your Thinking
3-4

Visual Thinking

The answers to the problems are the numbers for the dots.
Write the answers.
Connect the dots.

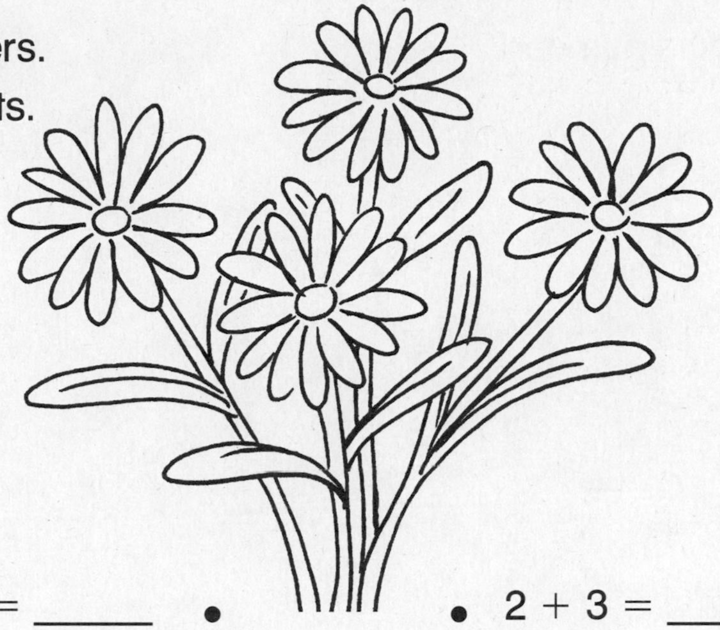

4 + 2 = ____ 2 + 3 = ____

3 + 4 = ____ 1 + 3 = ____

6 + 2 = ____ 3 + 0 = ____

4 + 5 = ____ 1 + 1 = ____

4 + 8 = ____

3 + 7 = ____ 5 + 6 = ____ 0 + 1 = ____

Notes for Home Your child completed addition sentences and used the answers as guides in completing a dot-to-dot picture. *Home Activity:* Ask your child to make up an addition story about the flowers in the vase.

Name _____

Critical Thinking

Read each clue and add.

Cross out the rabbit with that number.

What is the magic number?

1. It is not   4
             + 6
             10

2. It is not   7
             + 2

3. It is not   6
             + 6

4. It is not   5
             + 3

5. It is not   4
             + 2

6. It is not   1
             + 6

The magic number is _____.

Notes for Home Your child solved vertical addition problems and used clues to find the magic number.
Home Activity: Write the same addition problems horizontally (4 + 6 = ___), and ask your child to solve them.

Patterns in Numbers

An alien splits into 2 aliens every hour.
How many aliens will there be at the end of 4 hours?

At first, there is _____ alien.

After 1 hour . . .

. . . there are _____ aliens.

After 2 hours . . .

. . . there are _____ aliens.

After 3 hours . . .

. . . there are _____ aliens.

After 4 hours . . .

. . . there are _____ aliens.

Notes for Home Your child used the pictures to discover doubling and to answer a question. *Home Activity:* Ask your child to make up an addition sentence to show the number of aliens after 3 hours; after 4 hours. (Possible answers 2 + 6 = 8 and 8 + 8 = 16).

Patterns in Numbers

Find the patterns.
Fill in the missing numbers.

9	7	5
___	6	4
7	___	3
6	___	___

9	6	3
8	___	2
___	4	___

© Scott Foresman Addison Wesley 1

Notes for Home Your child identified patterns of numbers in charts and filled in the missing numbers to complete the charts. *Home Activity:* Ask your child to explain the patterns in both charts.

Name _____

Critical Thinking

Write the answers.

Cross out the animal that is different.

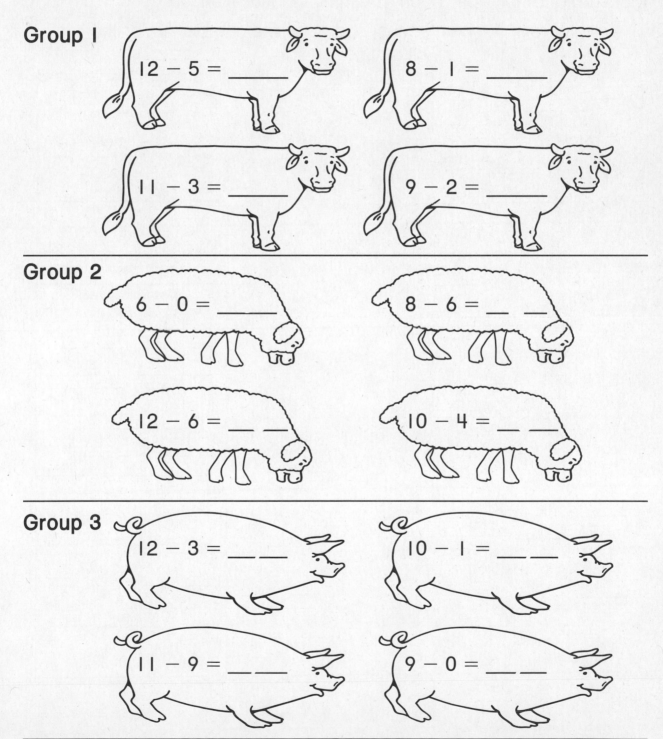

Group 1

12 − 5 = _____

8 − 1 = _____

11 − 3 = _____

9 − 2 = _____

Group 2

6 − 0 = _____

8 − 6 = _____

12 − 6 = _____

10 − 4 = _____

Group 3

12 − 3 = _____

10 − 1 = _____

11 − 9 = _____

9 − 0 = _____

Notes for Home Your child compared the answers to subtraction problems, and then crossed out the animal in each group with a different answer. *Home Activity:* Ask your child to identify the 2 crossed-out animals whose answers are the same.

Name _____

Decision Making

Make up a subtraction story about some of the
things in the box.

Make up another story about the things that are left.

The numbers in the boxes must add up to the number under the line.

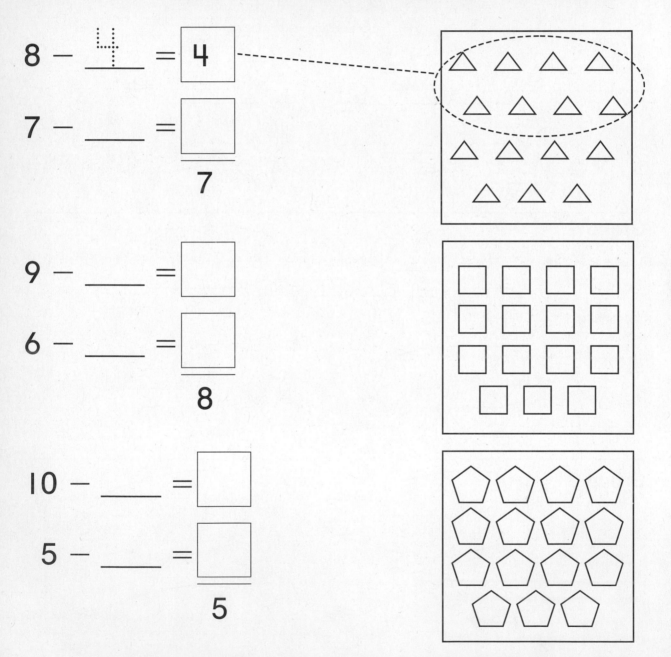

$8 - \underline{4} = \boxed{4}$

$7 - \underline{} = \boxed{}$

$\underline{7}$

$9 - \underline{} = \boxed{}$

$6 - \underline{} = \boxed{}$

$\underline{8}$

$10 - \underline{} = \boxed{}$

$5 - \underline{} = \boxed{}$

$\underline{5}$

Notes for Home Your child created pairs of subtraction number sentences whose answers added up to given numbers. *Home Activity:* Ask your child to explain how he or she chose numbers for the problems.

Critical Thinking

Subtract to find the correct answers.

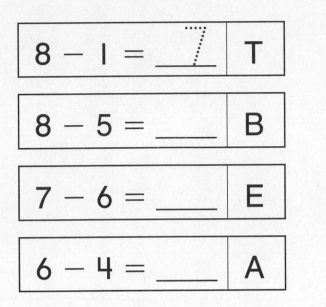

8 − 1 = __7__ | T

8 − 5 = ____ | B

7 − 6 = ____ | E

6 − 4 = ____ | A

9 − 4 = ____ | O

5 − 1 = ____ | P

9 − 3 = ____ | L

Look at the letters next to the answers.

Match the letters to the numbers on the lines below

to solve the riddles.

What has legs but cannot walk?

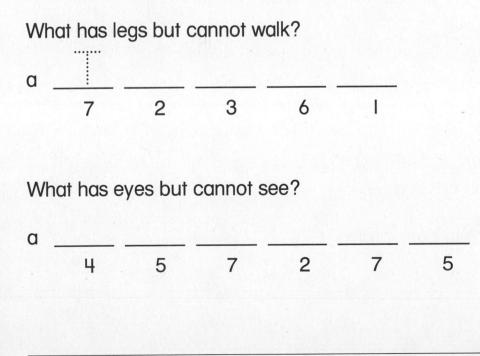

a __T__ ____ ____ ____ ____
    7   2   3   6   1

What has eyes but cannot see?

a ____ ____ ____ ____ ____ ____
    4   5   7   2   7   5

Notes for Home Your child solved subtraction problems and used letters that matched the answers to solve
riddles. *Home Activity:* Ask your child to write and solve the same subtraction problems in column format.

Visual Thinking

Circle things that hold water in red.

Circle things you use at meals in blue.

Some things will have only one circle.

Some things will have two circles.

How many things are in both circles? _____

Circle the squares in red.

Circle the shaded shapes in blue.

How many things are in both circles? _____

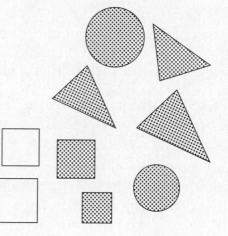

Circle things shaped like a ball in red.

Circle things that you eat in blue.

How many things are in both circles? _____

Notes for Home Your child drew circles to show where things belong. *Home Activity:* Ask your child to explain each drawing.

Name _____

Decision Making

Read the problem.

Write + or − and the answer.

Write what the children can do.

10 children are at a party. 2 children leave.

10   2 =   What can they play? _____

_____

2 girls are outside. 1 girl comes over.

2   1 =   What can they play? _____

_____

6 children are camping. 2 children go home.

6   2 =   What can they do? _____

_____

1 boy has a ball. 1 boy joins him.

1   1 =   What can they play? _____

_____

© Scott Foresman Addison Wesley 1

Notes for Home Your child completed number sentences to match given situations, then described an activity that the children in the situation could enjoy. *Home Activity:* Ask your child to make up a situation like the ones on this page. Have him or her write a number sentence to match the story.

Visual Thinking

Play with a classmate. Take turns trying to get
from Start to End.

For each turn, toss a coin.

If it lands heads up, move 1 space by coloring 1 square
on your game board.

If it lands tails up, move 2 spaces by coloring two squares
on your game board.

Count as you jump. See who gets to the End first.

Notes for Home Your child counted on to find sums through 12. *Home Activity:* Ask your child how much is
4 and 3. (7)

Name _____

Critical Thinking

Complete the sentence for each child.

Jack: I have __6__ cars and Jill has __5__ cars. __6 + 5 = 11__

Jill: I have __5__ cars and Jack has _____ cars. _____

Rosa: I have __7__ brushes and Beth has __5__ brushes.

_____

Beth: I have _____ brushes and Rosa has _____ brushes.

_____

Mimi: I have _____ balloons and Don has _____ balloons.

_____

Don: I have __7__ 7 balloons and Mimi has __3__ 3 balloons.

_____

Luc: I have __9__ dogs and Sam has __3__ dogs. _____

Sam: I have _____ dogs and Luc has _____ dogs. _____

Notes for Home Your child wrote two different addition facts to describe the same number of objects.
Home Activity: Divide 11 spoons between you and your child and have your child make up two different addition sentences with the facts 8 and 3. (8 + 3 = 11; 3 + 8 = 11) Repeat with a different division of the spoons.

Name _____

Decision Making

Draw an animal with 2 heads and 3 legs.

Choose one of these shapes for the body.

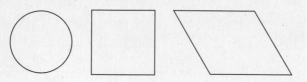

Use a different shape for the 2 heads.

Use the last shape for the 3 legs.

Write **1** in each body shape.

Write **2** in each head shape.

Write **3** in each leg shape.

Then write a number from your animal in each shape below.

Find the sums.

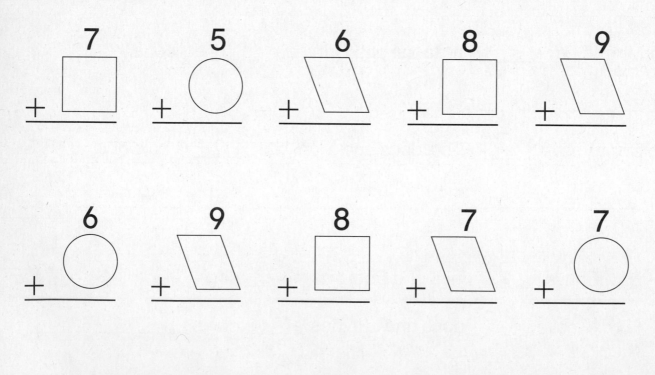

Notes for Home Your child found sums by adding 1, 2, or 3 to greater addends. *Home Activity:* Ask your child to find the sums of 9 + 3 (12), 8 + 3 (11), 6 + 3 (9), 9 + 2 (11), and 7 + 2 (9).

Patterns in Numbers

Draw what comes next in each pattern.

Show the pattern on the number line.

Write + 1, + 2, or + 3 on the line to the right.

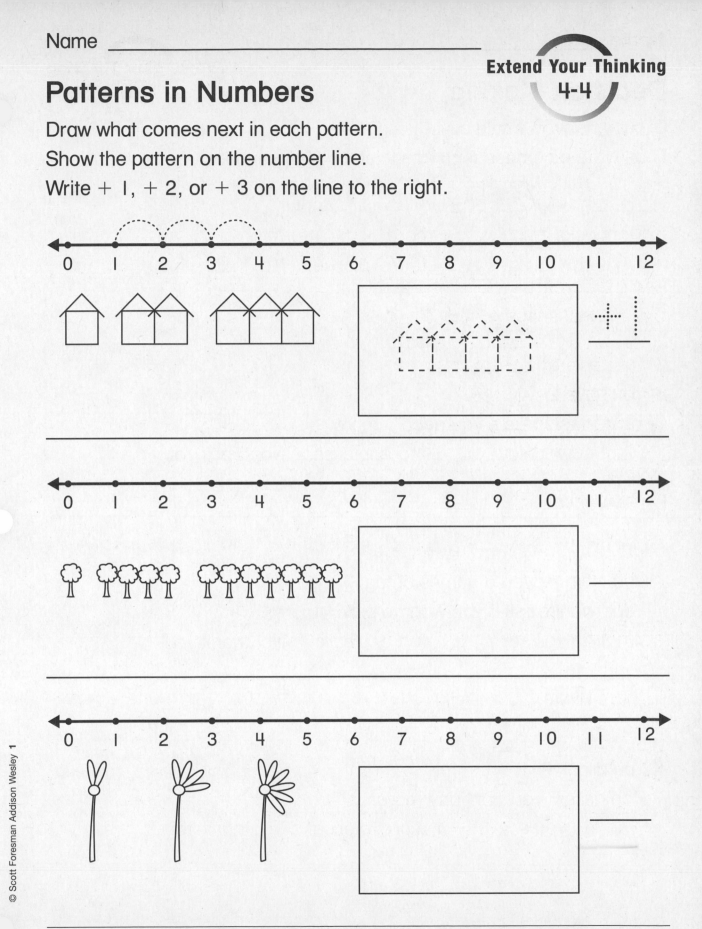

Notes for Home Your child used a number line to count on 1, 2 or 3 to discover patterns. *Home Activity:* Ask your child to draw the picture that would come next in one of the patterns.

© Scott Foresman Addison Wesley 1

Use with pages 139–140. **41**

Name _____

Decision Making

Circle what you would say.

Then write a number sentence to show what happens.

1. You ate 3  .

   Mom asks if you want 1 more.

   What do you say?   I more, please.   (No, thank you.)

   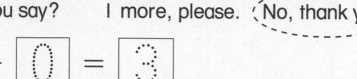

2. You have 2 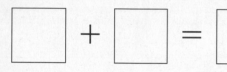 .

   Your friend asks if you need 1 more.

   What do you say?   I more, please.   No, thank you.

   ☐ + ☐ = ☐

3. You have played 6 games of tag.

   Your friends ask if you want to play 1 more.

   What do you say?   I more, please.   No, thank you.

   ☐ + ☐ = ☐

4. You drank 4 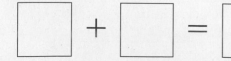 .

   Dad asks if you want any more.

   What do you say?   I more, please.   No, thank you.

   ☐ + ☐ = ☐

Notes for Home Your child found sums by adding zero or 1. *Home Activity:* Ask your child to explain his or her answers.

Visual Thinking

Write how many of each food is in the garden.
Find each sum.

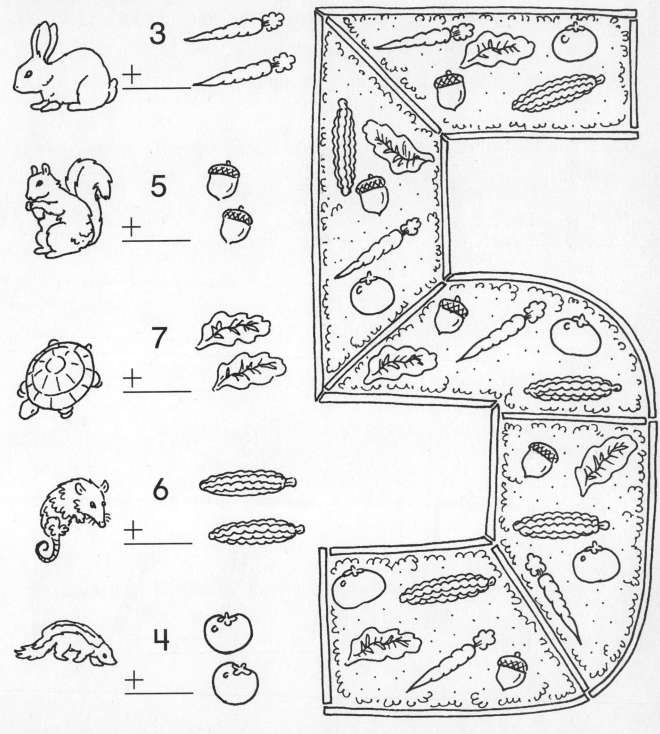

3
+ ___

5
+ ___

7
+ ___

6
+ ___

4
+ ___

© Scott Foresman Addison Wesley 1

Notes for Home Your child found sums with 5 as an addend. *Home Activity:* Ask your child to use his or her fingers to count on (forward) 5 to find the sum of a large number and 5, for example 87 + 5. (92)

Critical Thinking

Show the children to their seats.

Use the clues the children give you.

For each child, write his or her name below the correct seat.

Lee: My seat number is less than 12 and more than 10.

Laura: My seat number is more than 6 and less than 10.
It is even.

Kim: My seat number is more than 8 and less than 11.
It is odd.

Stacy: My seat number is more than 9 and less than 12.
It is even.

Robert: My seat number is less than 9 and more than 6.
It is odd.

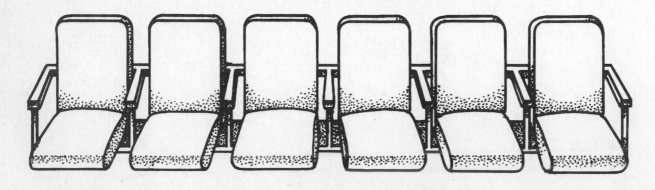

Notes for Home Your child used logical thinking to discover unknown numbers. *Home Activity:* Ask your child to guess a number you have chosen. Give him or her clues like the ones on this page which will lead to one correct answer.

Name _____

Decision Making

Everyone must be off when the elevator
gets to the bottom!
Only 0, 1, or 2 people get off at each floor.
At each stop, fill in the boxes and circles.

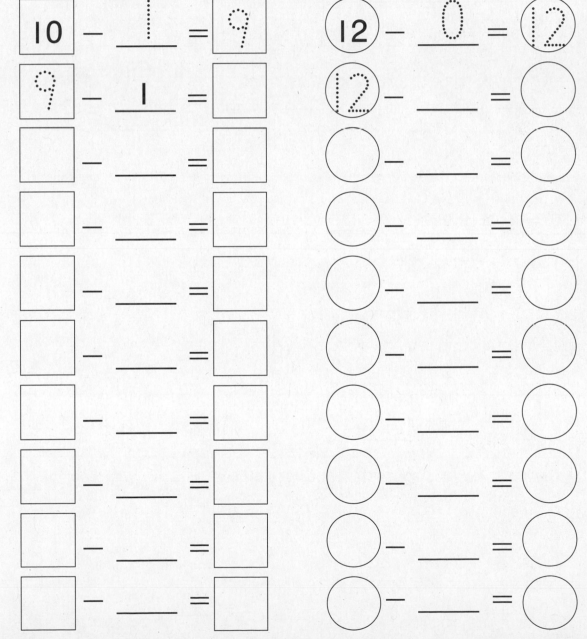

Floors   People

| 10 − 1 = 9 | | 12 − 0 = 12 |

9 − 1 = ☐   12 − ☐ = ◯

© Scott Foresman Addison Wesley 1

Notes for Home Your child subtracted 0, 1, or 2 from 12 and numbers below 12. *Home Activity:* Ask your child to read the subtraction sentences aloud in the People column.

Visual Thinking

What did Mama Bear say to Billy Bear?

Here's how to find out.

Solve each problem. Write the answer.

Match the answer to a letter from the list.

Write the letter on the line.

A = 1	F = 4	N = 7	U = 10
D = 2	H = 5	O = 8	V = 11
E = 3	K = 6	R = 9	W = 12

W
12 – 0 = $\underline{12}$ 9 – 1 = ___   11 – 2 = ___   7 – 1 = ___

7 – 2 = ___   1 – 0 = ___   10 – 1 = ___   4 – 2 = ___

6 – 1 = ___   3 – 2 = ___   12 – 1 = ___   5 – 2 = ___

6 – 2 = ___   11 – 1 = ___   9 – 2 = ___

Notes for Home Your child counted back by 0, 1, or 2 to solve subtraction facts and matched answers to letters to crack a code. *Home Activity:* For one of the given number sentences, ask your child to think of another number sentence that would have the same answer. For example, for 9 – 2 = 7, an alternate might be 8 – 1 = 7.

Name _____

Visual Thinking

Find the differences.

If you subtract 0, color that part of the pattern blue.

If the answer is 0, color that part of the pattern red.

If 0 is NOT in the problem at all, do not color that part.

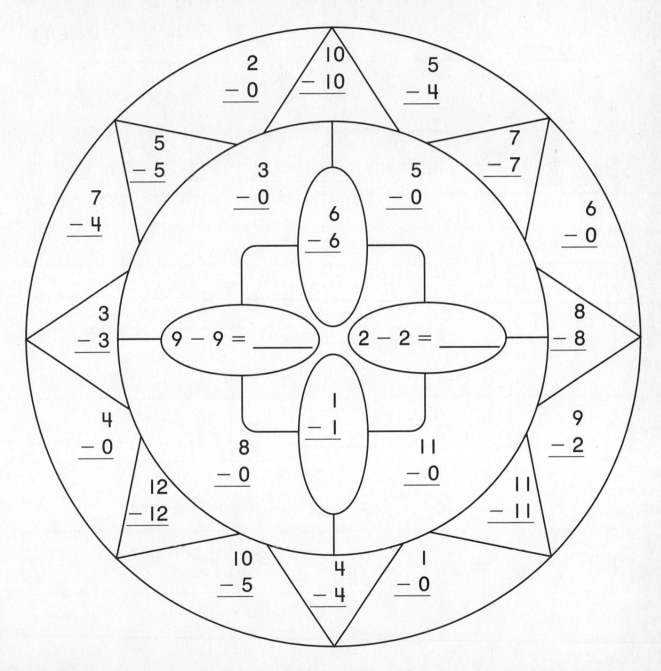

© Scott Foresman Addison Wesley 1

Notes for Home Your child found differences in facts involving 0. *Home Activity:* Ask your child to make up a story problem about one of the facts, such as "7 birds were in a bush. When I walked past, 7 birds flew away. How many were left?" (0)

Name _____

Critical Thinking

Extend Your Thinking
4-11

Write the missing numbers on each line.

In one fact in each row, you do not subtract 5.

Cross out that fact.

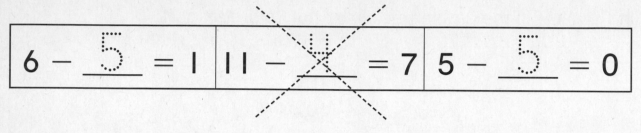

$6 - \underline{5} = 1$	$11 - \underline{\cancel{4}} = 7$	$5 - \underline{5} = 0$

$12 - \underline{} = 7$	$7 - \underline{} = 2$	$10 - \underline{} = 4$

$10 - \underline{} = 5$	$9 - \underline{} = 5$	$8 - \underline{} = 3$

$12 - \underline{} = 6$	$9 - \underline{} = 4$	$11 - \underline{} = 6$

$11 - \underline{} = 6$	$11 - \underline{} = 5$	$12 - \underline{} = 7$

Notes for Home Your child identified facts in which 5 was subtracted. *Home Activity:* Ask your child to draw an original picture to illustrate one of the facts that is not crossed off.

48 Use with pages 157–158.

Name _____

Critical Thinking

Write a subtraction number sentence for each picture.

Now draw your own picture.
Write a subtraction number
sentence.

Notes for Home Your child solved picture problems by writing number sentences. *Home Activity:* Ask your child to tell the story that goes along with his or her picture and number sentence.

Name _____

Patterns in Geometry

Circle each shelf that shows a pattern
without using the last shape.

Draw a line to the shape that comes next in each pattern.

Notes for Home Your child circled each row that shows a pattern of solid shapes. *Home Activity:* Ask your child to explain the difference between two geometric solids, for example, a sphere and a cylinder. (A sphere has no flat sides; a cylinder has 2 flat sides.)

Name _____

Visual Thinking

When you cut an orange, you can see a circle shape.

When you cut a log, one shape you can get is a rectangle.

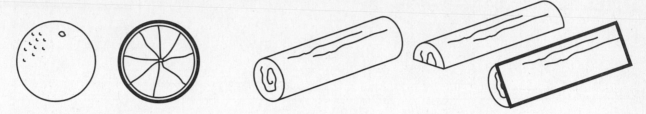

Cut each shape in two different ways. Draw the shapes
you might get with each cut.

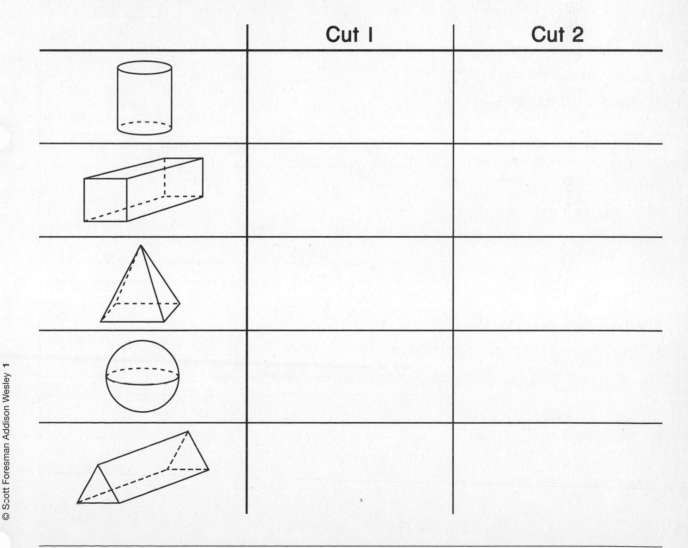

	Cut I	Cut 2

Notes for Home Your child identified plane shapes that would be formed on cut solids. *Home Activity:* Show your child a food with a distinct shape such as a cube of cheese, or a grapefruit. Cut it. Ask your child what shapes he or she sees at the cut surface.

Name _____

Critical Thinking

Help Ann sort these shapes.

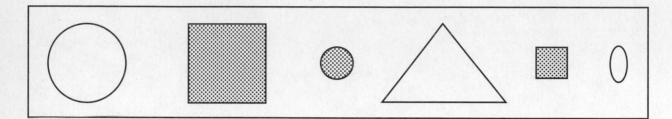

Draw the shapes in the correct boxes below.
Some shapes belong in 2 boxes.

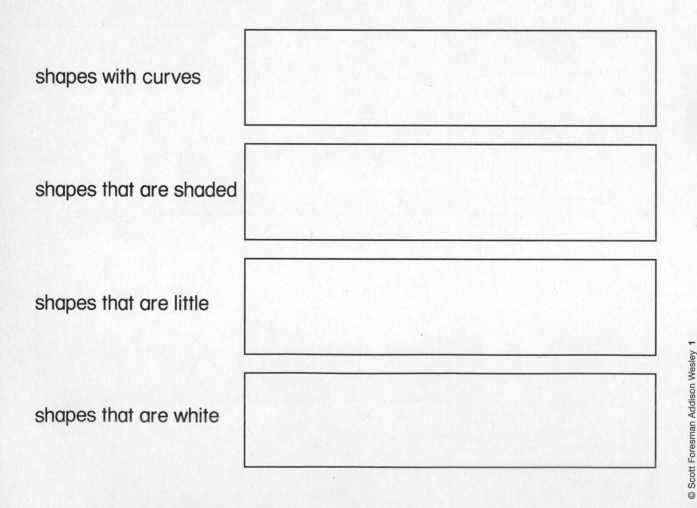

shapes with curves

shapes that are shaded

shapes that are little

shapes that are white

© Scott Foresman Addison Wesley 1

Notes for Home Your child sorted shapes in four different ways. *Home Activity:* Ask your child to draw four more shapes, one for each of the boxes.

Name _____

Visual Thinking

Do the following for each row.

Write S on the two figures with the same shape and size.

Write L on the little figure with the same shape.

Write D on the figure with a different shape.

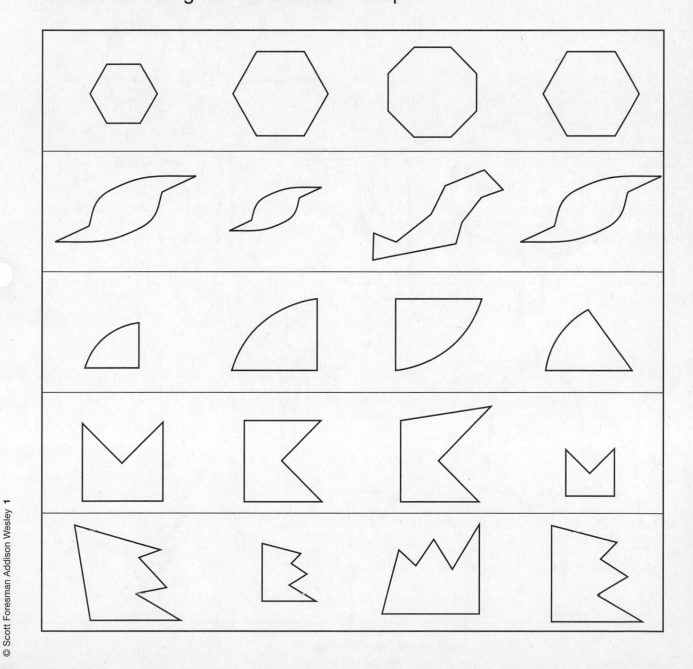

Notes for Home Your child identified figures that are the same size and shape, and identified figures that are the same shape but different size. *Home Activity:* Ask your child to draw two simple figures that are the same size and shape.

Name _____

Decision Making

Kevin is making special cards.

He wants to make them by folding paper in half and cutting.

Cross out the shapes he cannot make that way.

Draw and color to make each card look special.

Notes for Home Your child identified symmetrical shapes. *Home Activity:* Help your child fold a sheet of paper and cut it to make interesting shapes. Together, decorate each shape and make a collage by pasting the shapes onto another sheet of paper.

Name _____

Critical Thinking

Use the clues and the chart to find out who
owns which toys.

	CXDS	balls	stuffed animals	blocks
Lee	NO	YES	NO	NO
Bill				
Jean				

Lee's toys bounce.

Lee's row: Write YES under the toys that bounce.

Write NO under all the other toys.

Bill's toys have the same shape on every side.

Bill's row: Write NO under the toys that are Lee's.

Write NO under toys with a different shape on different sides.

Write YES under the toys that are left.

Jean's toys have corners.

Jean's row: Write NO under Lee's and Bill's toys.

Write NO under toys that do not have corners.

Write YES under the toys that are left.

© Scott Foresman Addison Wesley 1

Notes for Home Your child solved a problem by making a table. *Home Activity:* Ask your child to explain his or her reasons for deciding which toys were Bill's.

Visual Thinking

Linda and three friends are making birdhouses.

They have marked where Dad should cut.

Circle the things that they will share equally.

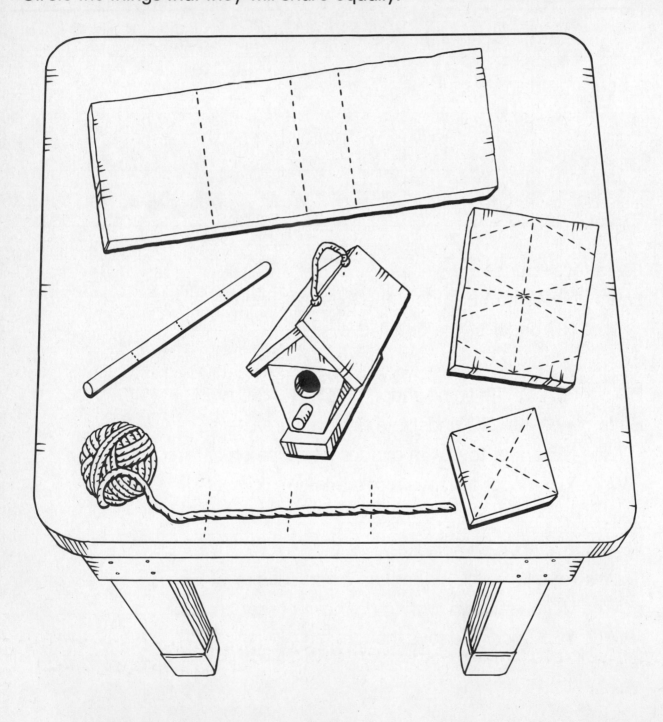

Notes for Home Your child identified things that were divided in four equal parts. *Home Activity:* Challenge your child to draw two lines to divide a circle into four equal parts.

Critical Thinking

John has a big oatmeal cookie.

He wants to share it equally with his friend.

Circle the picture that shows how he should cut it.

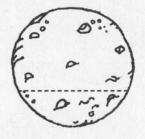

Beth has a small pizza.

She wants to share it equally with her friend.

Circle the picture that shows how she should cut it.

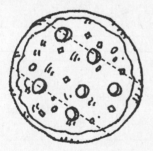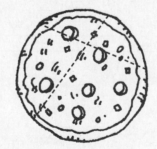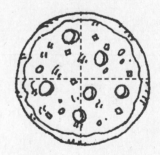

Sara has a piece of cloth.

She wants to share it equally with I friend.

Show ways she could cut it.

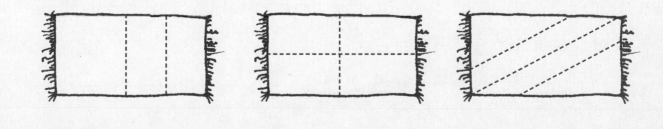

© Scott Foresman Addison Wesley 1

Notes for Home Your child identified shapes divided into halves and fourths. *Home Activity:* Challenge your child to divide a piece of construction paper into fourths. You might suggest that he or she fold the paper before drawing lines or cutting.

Name _____

Critical Thinking

Miguel and Evan want to share a sandwich.

How can they divide the sandwich into equal pieces?

Draw a picture to show how they share.

Draw a picture to help these children share.

1. The 3 children want to share a small pizza.

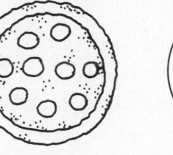 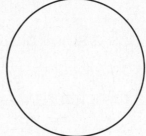

2. The 4 children want to share the bread.

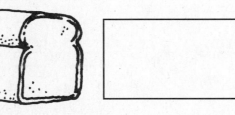

3. The 3 children want to share a waffle.

4. The 4 children want to share the sandwich.

© Scott Foresman Addison Wesley 1

Notes for Home Your child drew pictures to show how foods could be shared equally. *Home Activity:* Ask your child to draw a picture to show how you and he or she could share an orange, banana, or a piece of bread.

Name _____

Critical Thinking

Color all the shapes with 3 equal parts.

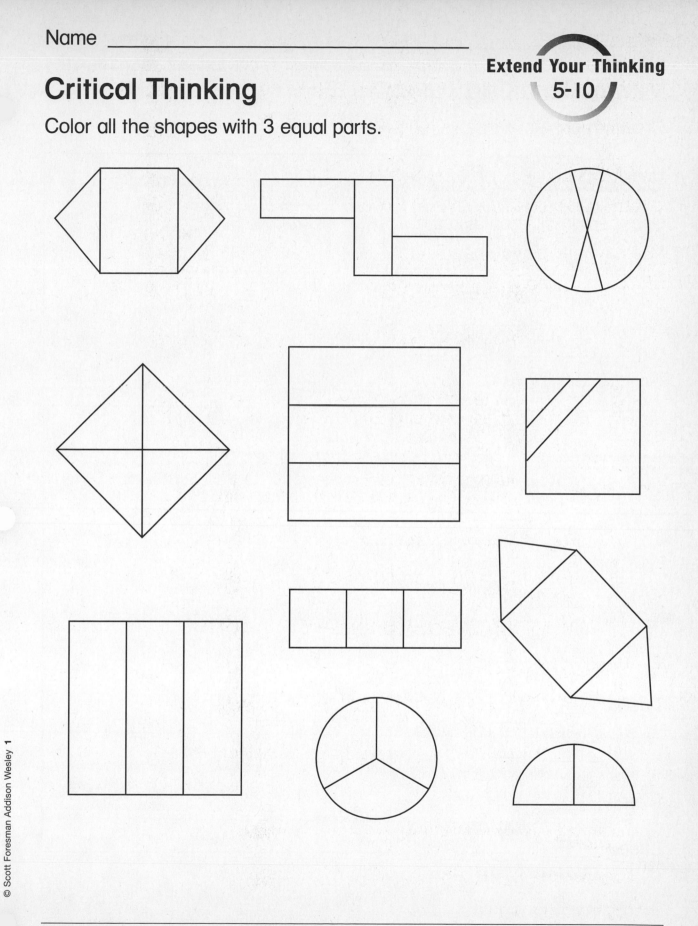

Notes for Home Your child colored the shapes with 3 equal parts. *Home Activity:* Ask your child to find a shape on the page with 2 equal parts; 4 equal parts.

Name _____

Visual Thinking

Draw a monster.

Use △ □ ○ ▭ .

Use them in different sizes.
Use as many as you need.

I used _____ △ .

I used _____ □ .

I used _____ ○ .

I used _____ ▭ .

Notes for Home Your child used triangles, squares, circles, and rectangles to create a drawing of an imaginary creature. *Home Activity:* Ask your child which shapes he or she used the most and the least.

Name _____

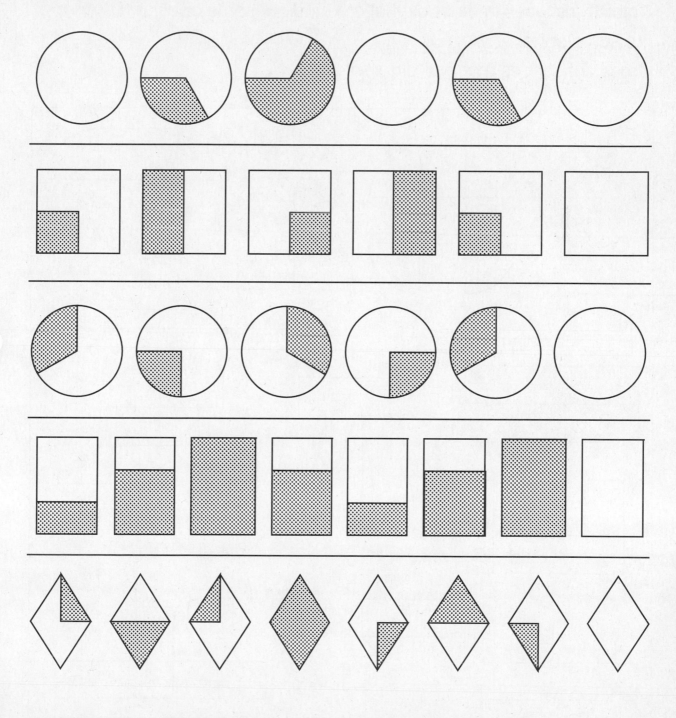

Patterns in Geometry

Find the pattern.

Color the last shape to extend the pattern.

Notes for Home Your child identified the pattern of fractional parts and wholes. *Home Activity:* Ask your child to explain one of the patterns to you. Then have your child point out the shapes that have 1/3 shaded. (First row-second and fifth shapes; third row-first, third, and fifth shapes; fourth row-first and fifth shapes.)

Visual Thinking

Look at how the first shape in each box is cut into parts.

Can the parts make a new shape?

Color the shapes in that box that are made of some or all of

the same parts.

Cross out shapes made of different parts.

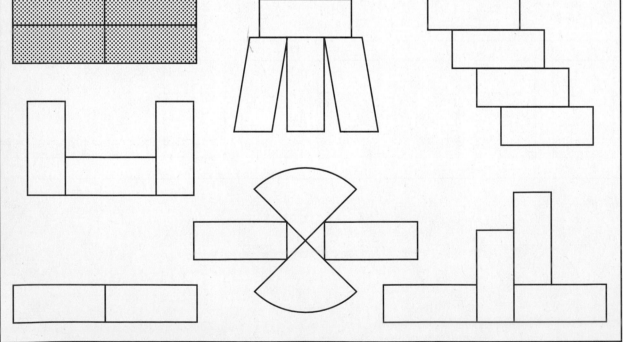

Notes for Home Your child identified shapes made of fractional parts of the first shape in each set. *Home Activity:* Encourage your child to trace the fractional parts of either shape to make a new shape.

Name _____

Decision Making

You are planning decorations for a party.

You may have one set or two sets of each decoration below.

Circle the fact that tells your choice.

Then complete the list.

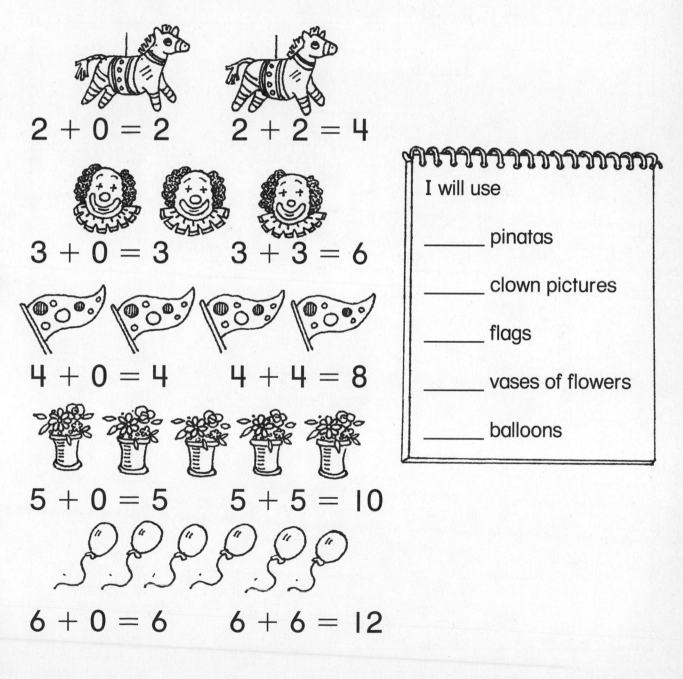

$2 + 0 = 2$ $2 + 2 = 4$

$3 + 0 = 3$ $3 + 3 = 6$

$4 + 0 = 4$ $4 + 4 = 8$

$5 + 0 = 5$ $5 + 5 = 10$

$6 + 0 = 6$ $6 + 6 = 12$

I will use

_____ pinatas

_____ clown pictures

_____ flags

_____ vases of flowers

_____ balloons

© Scott Foresman Addison Wesley 1

Notes for Home Your child chose single sets or doubles of items, circled related addition facts, and recorded the sums of the chosen items. *Home Activity:* Ask your child to locate and arrange these sets of doubles on a table: 2 sets of 3 glasses; 2 sets of 4 plates; 2 sets of 5 forks; 2 sets of 6 spoons.

Name _____

Visual Thinking

Solve all the problems.

Color each space that has a doubles fact red.

Color each space that has a doubles fact plus 1 green.

Color all other spaces brown.

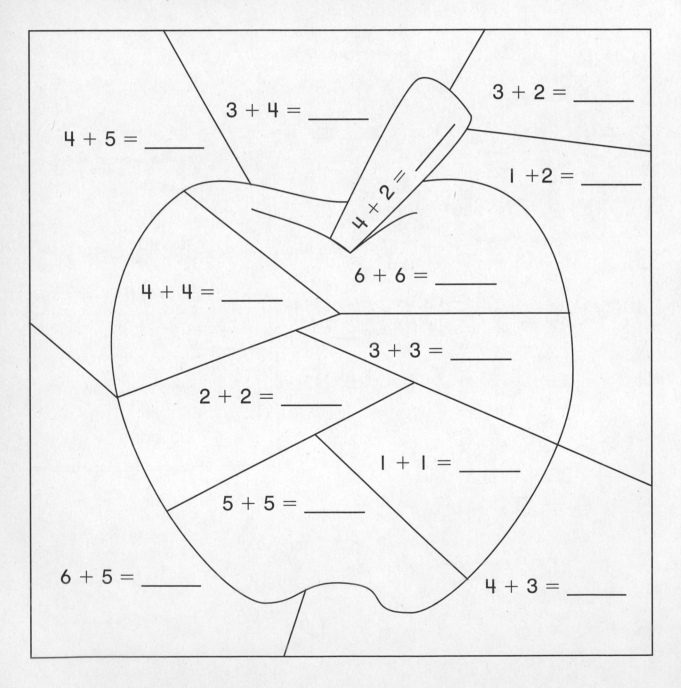

3 + 4 = _____

4 + 5 = _____

3 + 2 = _____

4 + 2 = _____

1 + 2 = _____

4 + 4 = _____

6 + 6 = _____

3 + 3 = _____

2 + 2 = _____

1 + 1 = _____

5 + 5 = _____

6 + 5 = _____

4 + 3 = _____

Notes for Home Your child solved facts to 12 and then colored spaces according to the descriptors above.
Home Activity: Ask your child to explain what a doubles fact is and to give one example. (Doubles facts include
1 + 1, 2 + 2, 3 + 3, and so on.)

Name _____

Critical Thinking

Solve each problem.

Circle the answers that show a doubles fact.

Box the answers that show a doubles fact plus 1.

1. Myra bought 6 erasers. Kathy bought the same amount.

   How many erasers do they have together? _____

2. Robert found 5 pennies. John found 6 pennies.

   How many pennies did they find in all? _____

3. Alice brought home 2 kittens. Grace brought home 4 more.

   How many kittens do they have at home now? _____

4. Mark jumped across 4 puddles. Laura jumped across
   3 other puddles. How many puddles did they jump in all?

   _____

5. Farmer Bob had some carrots. He fed Rigby Rabbit 2 carrots. He
   also fed Molly Mule 2 carrots. Now he has no carrots.

   How many carrots did Farmer Bob have? _____

Notes for Home Your child solved addition problems and identified doubles facts and doubles facts plus 1.
Home Activity: Ask your child to create another problem that illustrates a doubles fact plus 1.
(For example: 3 + 4 = 7.)

Name ______________________________

Extend Your Thinking
6-4

Decision Making

Solve the addition facts. Read the problem.
Circle the addition doubles fact that helps solve each problem.
Then write the subtraction fact that answers each problem.

1. 3 + 3 = _____   4 + 4 = _____   5 + 5 = _____

   Frank stood on his head for 5 seconds.

   Rick stood on his head for 10 seconds.

   How much longer did Rick stand on his head?

   ____

2. 6 + 6 = _____   4 + 4 = _____   8 + 8 = _____

   Myra did 8 jumping jacks. Nan did 4.

   How many more did Myra do? ______________________________

____

Create your own problem to match 1 of the addition doubles facts shown below. Write a subtraction fact to go with the story.

5 + 5 = _____   6 + 6 = _____   3 + 3 = _____

On Tuesday, I ________________. I did this _____ times.

On Wednesday, I did it _____ times.

How many more times did I do it on ________________ than on

________________? _____ − _____ = _____

Notes for Home Your child used addition doubles facts to help solve word problems involving subtraction.
Home Activity: Ask your child to create another problem for you to solve.

Critical Thinking

Mr. Johnson's class voted on the place the children most
wanted to visit.

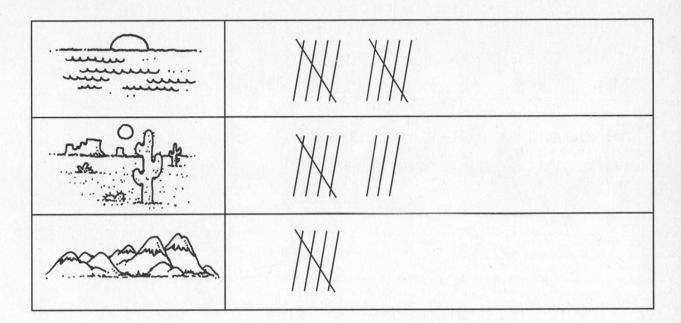

1. Which place do the most children want to visit? _____

2. How many children in this class live near the ~~~~~~?

_____

3. How many more children voted to visit the

than the _____? _____

4. Which place gets the least visitors every year?

_____

5. How many children would like to visit the _____? _____

Notes for Home Your child decided whether a given set of data would help answer related questions.
Home Activity: Ask your child to explain why the questions can or cannot be answered using only the data given
on the chart.

Visual Thinking

You need a coin and a marker.

Put your marker on START. Toss the coin.

Heads: Go to the next fact with all 3 numbers the same
as on the space with your marker.

Tails: Go to the next fact with at least 1 different number.

Move your marker. Repeat until you get to the END.

How many turns did you need to get to END? _____ turns.

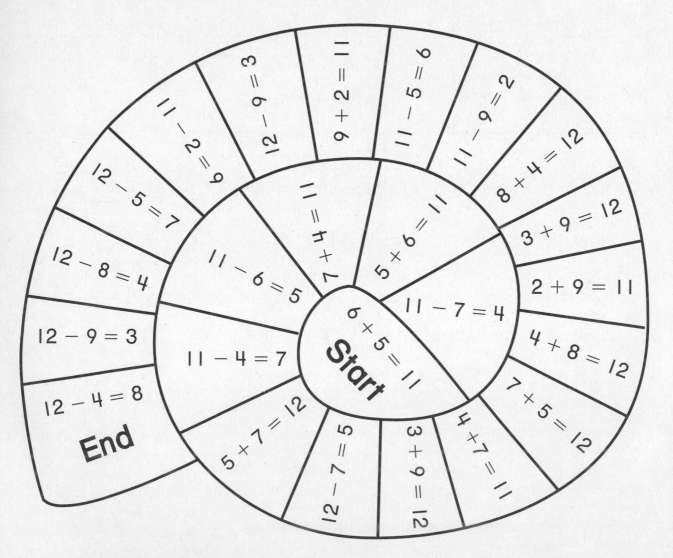

© Scott Foresman Addison Wesley 1

Notes for Home Your child identified related facts by moving his or her marker along a game board.
Home Activity: Ask your child to state related subtraction facts for these addition facts: 3 + 3 = 6 (6 − 3 = 3),
4 + 4 = 8 (8 − 4 = 4), and 5 + 5 = 10 (10 − 5 = 5).

Critical Thinking

The fact families are having a picnic.

Color the ones that belong to this family [brown] : 6 + 5 = 11.

Color the ones that belong to this family [orange] : 4 + 8 = 12.

Color the ones that belong to this family [gray] : 10 − 3 = 7.

5 + 6 = 11

11 − 6 = 5

11 − 5 = 6

12 − 4 = 8

8 + 4 = 12

12 − 8 = 4

7 + 3 = 10

10 − 7 = 3

3 + 7 = 10

© Scott Foresman Addison Wesley 1

Notes for Home Your child identified members of fact families up to 12. *Home Activity:* Ask your child if each fact family has more or fewer members than his or her own family. (There are 4 members in each fact family.)

Name _____

Patterns in Numbers

Add to fill in the missing numbers in the chart.

Number	+ 1	+ 2	+ 3	+ 4	+ 5
6	7	8	(9)		
7	8	(9)	10		
8	(9)	10	11		13
9	10			13	14

Use the chart to subtract.

1. 9 − 3 = ____
   (1) Circle each 9 in red.
   (2) Underline the 9 under +**3**.
   (3) What number is furthest to

   the left in that row? _____

2. 13 − 5 = ____
   (1) Circle each 13 in blue.
   (2) Underline the 13 under +**5**.
   (3) What number is furthest to

   the left? _____

3. 10 − 3 = ____
   (1) Circle each 10 in green.
   (2) Underline the 10 under +**3**.
   (3) What number is 3 squares

   to the left? _____

4. 14 − 5 = ____
   (1) Circle each 14 in orange.
   (2) Underline the 14 under +**5**.
   (3) What number is 5 squares

   to the left? _____

5. 12 − 3 = ____

6. 12 − 4 = ____

Notes for Home Your child completed a grid using addition and then used the grid to answer subtraction problems. *Home Activity:* Ask your child to use the grid to work these problems: 10 − 1 = (9), 11 − 5 = (6), 13 − 4 = (9).

Critical Thinking

Solve the addition problems.

Draw lines to match each addition problem
with a related subtraction fact.

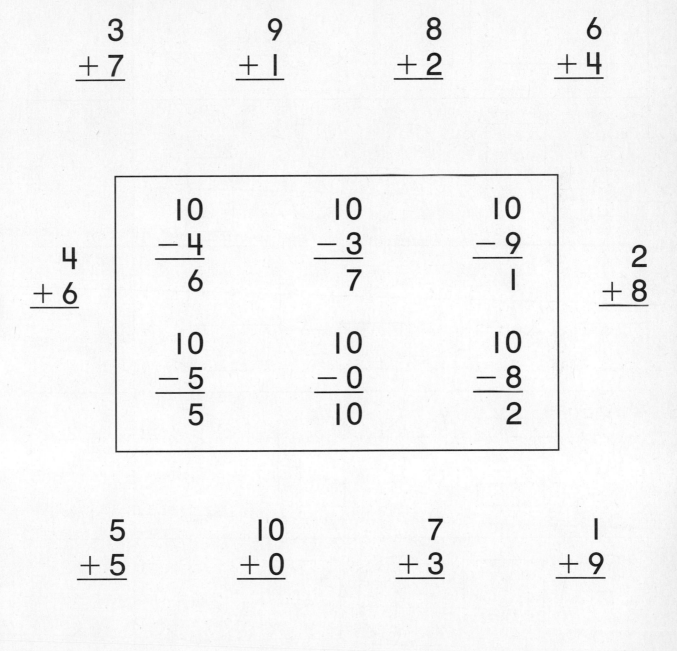

$$\begin{array}{r} 3 \\ +7 \\ \hline \end{array}$$
$$\begin{array}{r} 9 \\ +1 \\ \hline \end{array}$$
$$\begin{array}{r} 8 \\ +2 \\ \hline \end{array}$$
$$\begin{array}{r} 6 \\ +4 \\ \hline \end{array}$$

$$\begin{array}{r} 4 \\ +6 \\ \hline \end{array}$$

$$\begin{array}{r} 10 \\ -4 \\ \hline 6 \end{array}$$
$$\begin{array}{r} 10 \\ -3 \\ \hline 7 \end{array}$$
$$\begin{array}{r} 10 \\ -9 \\ \hline 1 \end{array}$$

$$\begin{array}{r} 10 \\ -5 \\ \hline 5 \end{array}$$
$$\begin{array}{r} 10 \\ -0 \\ \hline 10 \end{array}$$
$$\begin{array}{r} 10 \\ -8 \\ \hline 2 \end{array}$$

$$\begin{array}{r} 2 \\ +8 \\ \hline \end{array}$$

$$\begin{array}{r} 5 \\ +5 \\ \hline \end{array}$$
$$\begin{array}{r} 10 \\ +0 \\ \hline \end{array}$$
$$\begin{array}{r} 7 \\ +3 \\ \hline \end{array}$$
$$\begin{array}{r} 1 \\ +9 \\ \hline \end{array}$$

Notes for Home Your child solved addition problems to 10 and matched them with subtraction facts.
Home Activity: Ask your child to write the subtraction fact for an addition problem to 9, such as 5 + 4 = 9.
(9 − 4 = 5)

Name _____

Patterns in Geometry

Draw what comes next in each row.

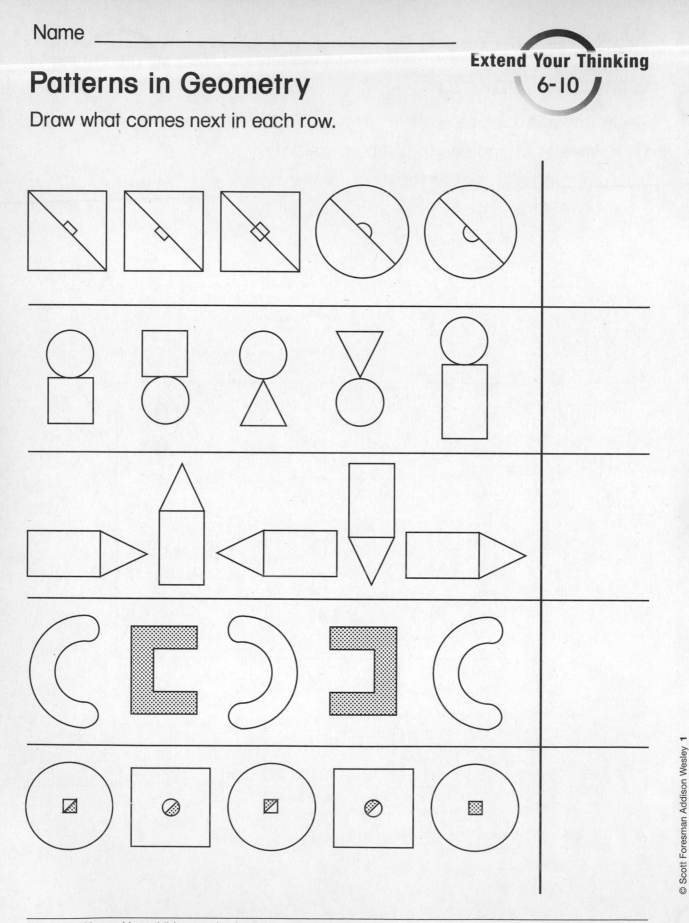

Notes for Home Your child recognized patterns of shapes and drew the shape that comes next in each pattern. *Home Activity:* Ask your child to explain one of the patterns.

Name _____

Visual Thinking

Both monkeys started walking home with 10 bananas.
As they walked, they got more bananas.
Follow their paths. Write how many bananas
each monkey had when they got home.
Circle the monkey who ended up with more.

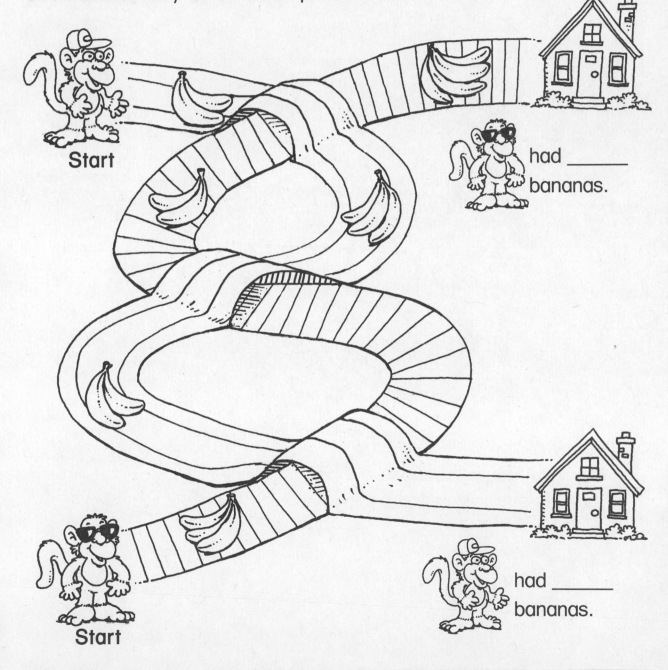

Start

had _____ bananas.

Start

had _____ bananas.

___

Notes for Home Your child used a picture to count on from 10 objects, and wrote numbers in the teens.
Home Activity: Ask your child to count by ones from 10 to 20.

Name _____

Visual Thinking

Add the stars in the center to the stars around it.

Write the sums in the outer circle.

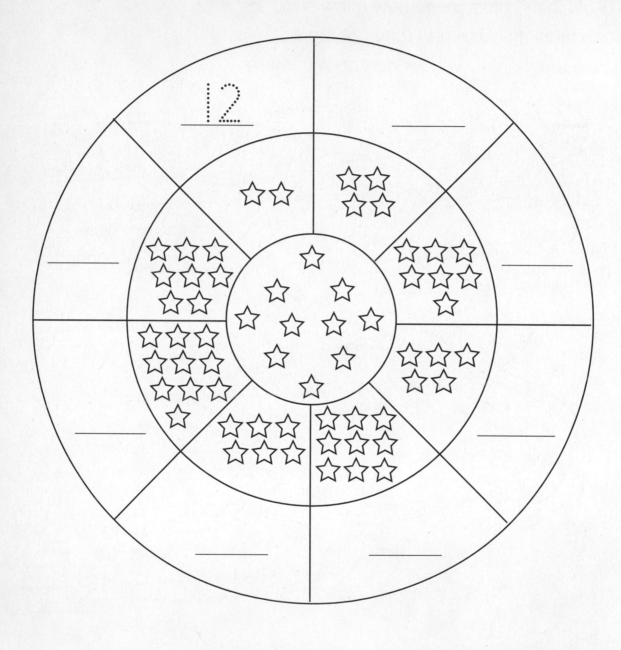

Notes for Home Your child counted groups to 20, using a group of 10 as the starting point. *Home Activity:* Help your child recreate this circle using dry beans. Together, count the 10 beans in the center and add them to the beans in each outer section.

Name _____

Decision Making

Each bus can take 20 children on the field trip.

Some groups are already on the buses.

Which group or groups can still get on each bus?

Draw lines between the group or groups and the bus.

10 children are on Bus A.   15 children are on Bus B.   5 children are on Bus C.

A   B   C

Notes for Home Your child identified ways to describe 20 as groups of 5, 10, and 20. *Home Activity:* Ask your child to describe another way to assign the groups to the buses.

Critical Thinking

Each child took a number from the hat.
What is each child's number?
Read the clues and write the numbers.

My number has 4 tens and 4 extras. _____

My number has 2 tens and 3 extras. _____

My number has some tens and 7 extras. _____

My number has 5 tens and 8 extras. _____

My number has 3 tens and some extras. _____

My number has 2 tens and some extras. _____

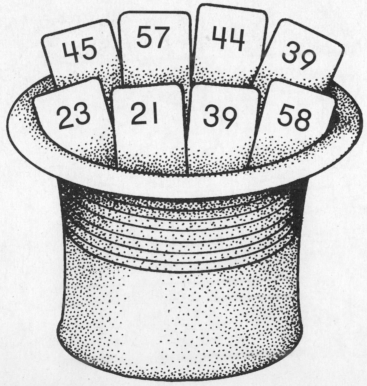

© Scott Foresman Addison Wesley 1

Notes for Home Your child identified groups of ten plus extras. *Home Activity:* Ask your child to find the two numerals that were not used (21 and 45) and tell how many tens and extras are in each. (21: 2 tens and 1 extra; 45: 4 tens and 5 extras)

Name _____

Decision Making

Help the library decide which kinds of books to buy.

This graph shows how many times books were taken out.

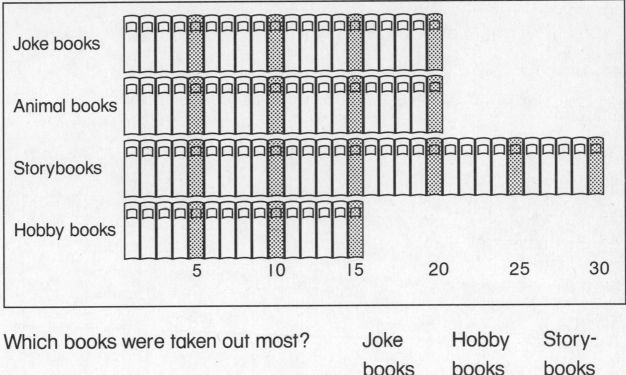

Which books were taken out most?

Joke	Hobby	Story-
books	books	books

Which books were taken out least?

Animal	Hobby	Joke
books	books	books

What kinds of books should the library buy?

Write 1 under the kind of book the library should buy first.

Write 2 and 3 under your next two choices.

Write 4 under the kind the library should buy last.

Joke books   Animal books   Storybooks   Hobby books

_____   _____   _____   _____

© Scott Foresman Addison Wesley 1

Notes for Home Your child used the information in a graph to solve a problem. *Home Activity:* Ask your child to explain the reasons for his or her ranking of the books.

Name _____

Critical Thinking

These graphs show what children did in a 60-yard hop-and-skip race.

The gray boxes show how far each racer hopped.

The white boxes show how far each racer skipped.

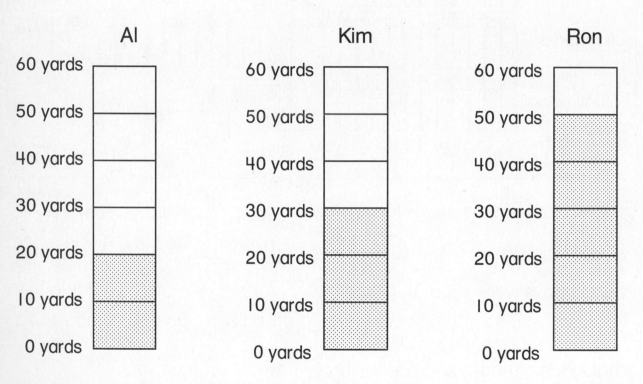

Use the graphs to answer these questions.

Al hopped _____ yards. Al skipped _____ yards.

Al hopped _____ yards + skipped _____ yards = 60 yards

Kim hopped _____ yards + skipped _____ yards = 60 yards

Ron hopped _____ yards + skipped _____ yards = 60 yards

Notes for Home Your child interpreted bar graphs and counted groups to 60. *Home Activity:* Ask your child to trace one of the graphs and fill in boxes to show this child's results: Luis hopped 40 yards. Then ask your child to tell how far Luis skipped. (20 yards)

Name _____

Visual Thinking

Count by 10s to connect the squares.

Count by 10s to connect the triangles.

Count by 2s to connect the dots.

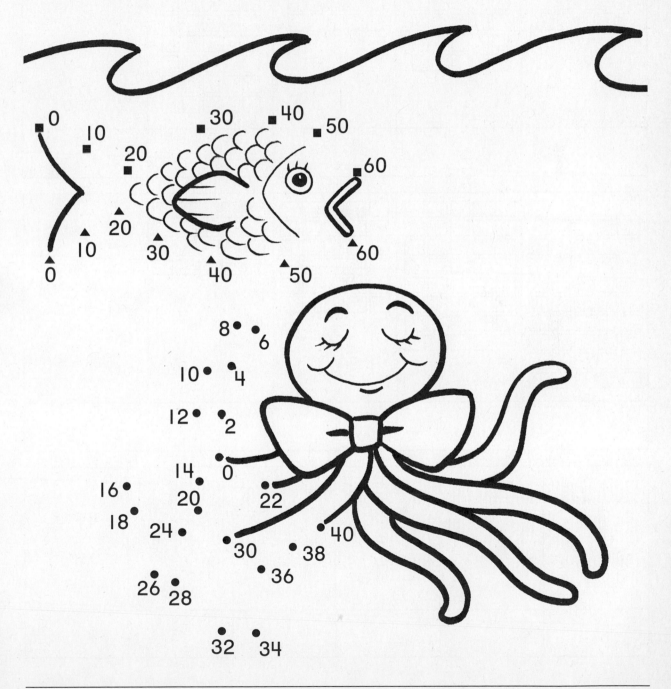

Notes for Home Your child counted by 2s and by 10s to complete dot-to-dot pictures. *Home Activity:* Ask your child to count backwards by 2s from 40 to 0.

Patterns in Numbers

Write how many shapes are in each box.

Find the pattern in each row.

Write the number and draw the shapes in the last box.

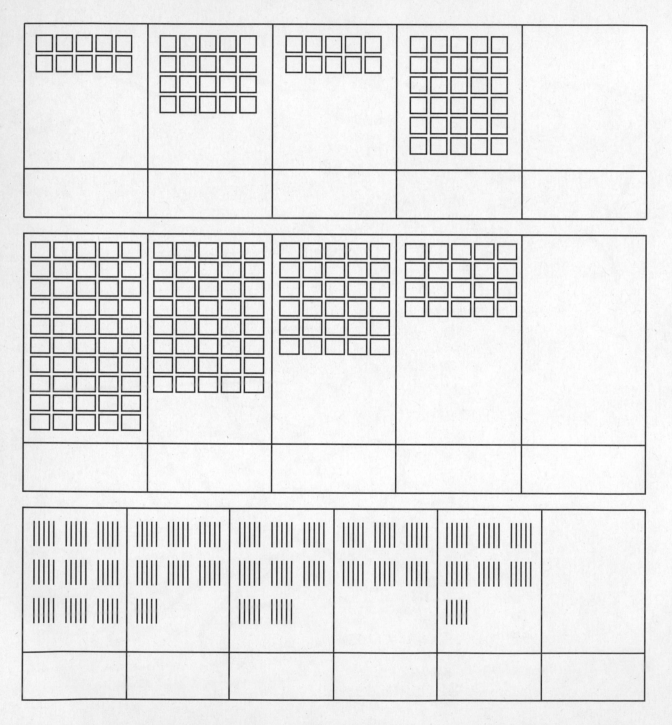

Notes for Home Your child counted shapes by 10s and 5s to identify and extend number patterns. *Home Activity:* Challenge your child to count from 10 to 60 forward and backward by 10s. (10, 20, 30, 40, 50, 60; 60, 50, 40, 30, 20, 10)

Name _____

Critical Thinking

Circle the letter that matches with the word in each row.

Then write it on the line below.

You will find out the answer to this riddle.

What time is it when the clock strikes 13?

second	T	(G)	U	R	L	I	D	P	Q	H
fourth	M	C	L	E	D	L	O	X	T	W
third	I	V	T	K	M	D	S	A	W	R
seventh	J	B	L	D	U	X	A	K	O	U
fifth	K	P	F	R	N	K	H	Y	U	D
sixth	L	M	B	C	R	E	L	G	T	B
ninth	D	W	I	N	G	K	Y	V	W	K
tenth	P	X	K	N	M	D	Y	G	L	C
eighth	F	E	K	N	C	X	Z	L	U	N
first	O	H	S	Q	I	M	Y	V	F	R
fifth	P	J	F	U	C	L	R	N	X	W
tenth	I	R	H	D	M	V	L	S	P	K

Time to G___ ___ ___   ___ ___ ___ ___ ___

___ ___ ___ ___ ___ ___

Notes for Home Your child followed directions involving ordinal position through tenth. *Home Activity:* Ask your child who was born first, second, third, and so on in your family.

Patterns in Numbers

Pat's school is putting a new path in its garden.

The path will have 30 stepping stones.

The parents will give money for every third stone.

  Write **P** on every third stone.

The children will give money for every fifth stone.

  Write **C** on every fifth stone.

Some stones will get money from both groups.

START

1. How many stones will the parents pay for by themselves? _____

2. How many stones will the children pay for by themselves? _____

3. How many stones will the two groups pay for together? _____

© Scott Foresman Addison Wesley 1

Notes for Home Your child solved a problem by identifying a pattern. *Home Activity:* Help your child count aloud by 3s to identify the number of each stepping stone marked with P.

Visual Thinking

This is the front of a card.   This is written on the back.

Draw lines to match the front and back of each card.

68

23

75

24

32

54

86

Notes for Home Your child matched pictures showing tens and ones with corresponding numerals. *Home Activity*: Ask your child to draw the front of the card for the number 75. (There should be 7 tens and 5 ones.)

Name _____

Critical Thinking

How many gold pieces is each elf bringing home?

Write the number of gold pieces on the elf's card.

Draw a line to show which door he should enter.

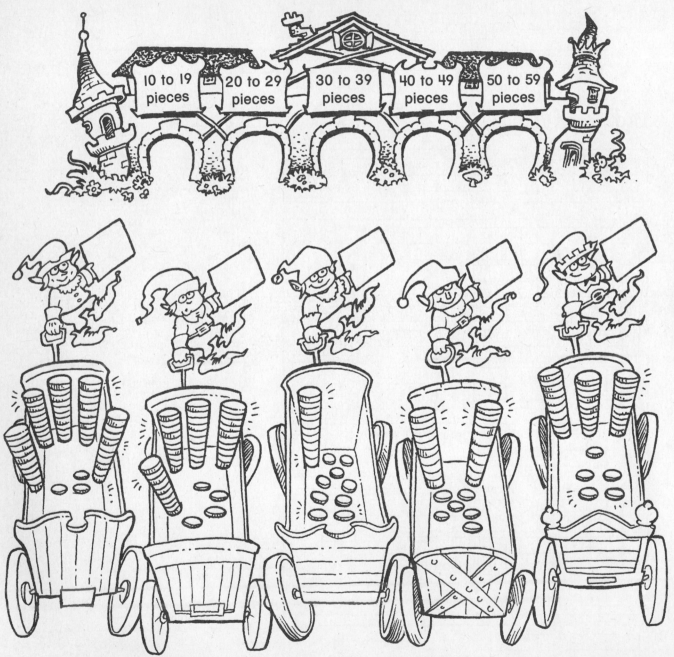

Notes for Home Your child wrote the correct 2-digit numbers for amounts between 10 and 60, and drew a line from each number to the correct tens range. *Home Activity:* Point out two elves and ask your child how many gold pieces each would have if one elf gave the other elf one of his piles of 10.

Name _____

Visual Thinking

Harry and Carrie took a walk.

They wanted to be sure to get back home so

they dropped a cherry after every 10 steps to mark their way.

After each rest, they counted on from one.

How many steps did the children take between each

of these places?

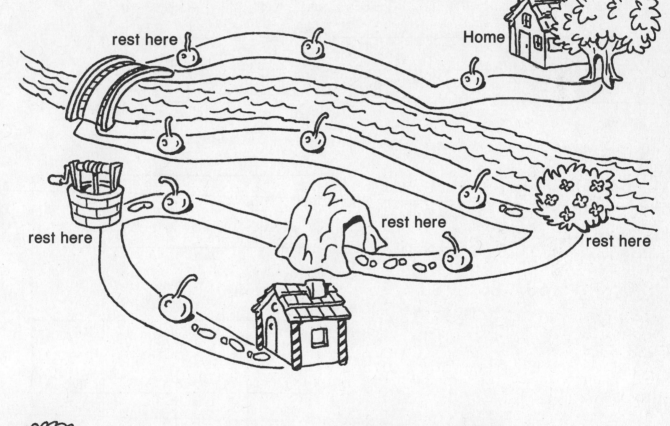

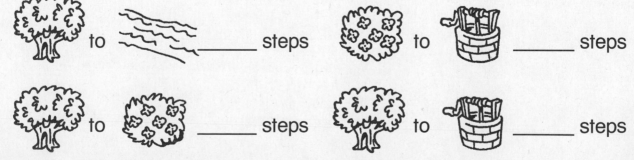

_____ to 〰〰〰 _____ steps   🌸 to 🪣 _____ steps

_____ to 🌸 _____ steps   🌳 to 🪣 _____ steps

© Scott Foresman Addison Wesley 1

Notes for Home Your child counted by groups of ten from 0 to 100. *Home Activity:* Help your child to find the
total distance from the beginning point (the hollow tree) to the house. (93 steps)

Decision Making

Lori will sew beads on this pattern.

10 beads fit in each whole square.

About how many beads will Lori need?

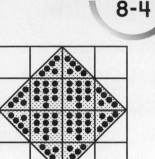

20   40   60   (80)   100

Sam has only 20 beads.

Circle the pattern Sam should use.

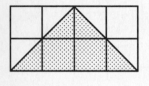   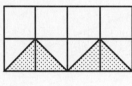   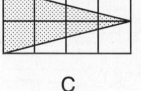

    A   B   C

Draw a pattern.

About how many beads will it use?

Circle the closest ten.

20   40   60   80   100

Notes for Home Your child estimated and counted by groups of 10 to 100. *Home Activity:* Ask your child to explain how he or she found the number of beads needed for each of Sam's possible patterns.

Critical Thinking

These children get 1 point for each good deed they do.

When a child gets 10 points, he or she gets a star.

Each \ means 1 point.

Each ☆ = 10 tally points.

Circle the children who will get a star for 1 more good deed.

Circle the children who will get a star for 2 more good deeds.

Circle the children who will get a star for 1 more good deed.

Notes for Home Your child decided when points could be traded for a star. *Home Activity:* Ask your child to figure out how many good deeds some of the children pictured above had done.

Name _____

Critical Thinking

You can use this machine to help you count.

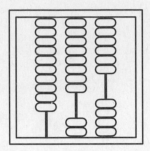

Here it shows the number 24.   Here it shows the number 38.

What number does each of these machines show?

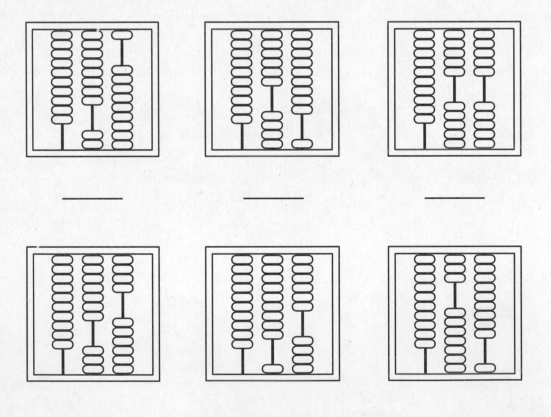

_____   _____   _____

_____   _____   _____

Notes for Home Your child interpreted the arrangements of beads on an abacus and then wrote the related numerals. *Home Activity:* Ask your child what the number 100 would look like on the abacus. (One bead down in the left column and all beads up in the other columns.)

Name _____

Critical Thinking

These aliens have a message, but it is out of order.

Put their numbers in the right order to see what the letters spell.

89 C	41 C	23 W	67 I	90 E
69	24 E	86 P	43 M	88 A
68 N	25	87 E	42 O	44 E

23 W						

Notes for Home Your child arranged numbers in numerical order to decode a message. *Home Activity:* Help your child use the numbers to write his or her own secret message.

Name _____

Decision Making

You are planning a party.

Keep these rules in mind as you plan.
Circle the answer you choose for each question.

1. You can have more than 10 and less than 19 guests.

   How many will you have?   18   23   9   12

2. You can spend more than 40 and less than 60 minutes
   playing games.

   How long will you play games?   30   45   59   70

3. You can give away less than 32 and more than 21 prizes.

   How many will you give away?   29   38   17   22

4. You can get more than 10 but less than 20 gifts.

   How many will you get?   11   24   19   35

5. You can play less than 15 but more than 9 games.

   How many will you play?   10   17   14   18

Notes for Home Your child planned a party, making choices involving numbers greater than some given numbers and less than others. *Home Activity:* Ask your child to explain his or her choices for the party.

Name _____

Patterns in Numbers

Many numbers are missing from this 100 chart.

Some pictures are in their places.

Fill in the rest of the chart.

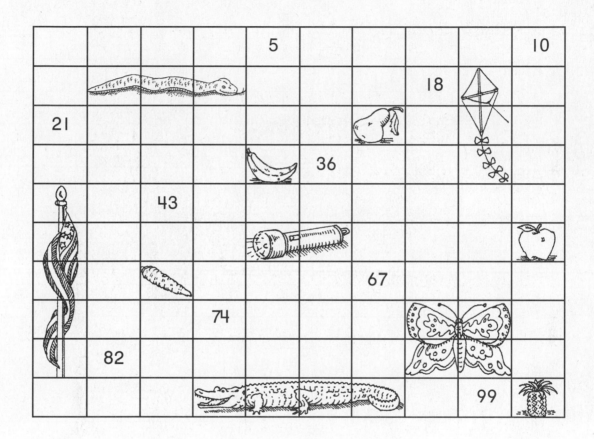

Match each picture with a number or with one of the

numbers it is covering.

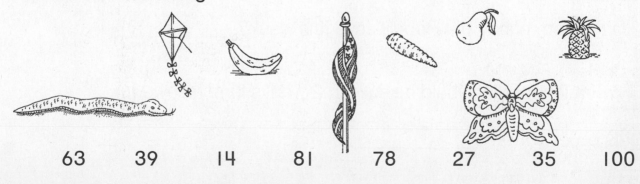

63   39   14   81   78   27   35   100

Notes for Home Your child identified the numerals that belong in the spaces of a 100 chart by matching numerals with pictures shown in their spaces. *Home Activity:* Ask your child to name the picture in the 60 space and the 2 numerals that belong where the flashlight is. (apple; 55 and 56)

© Scott Foresman Addison Wesley 1

Name _____

Patterns in Data

Robert saved money every day for 1 week.

This graph shows how much he saved each day.

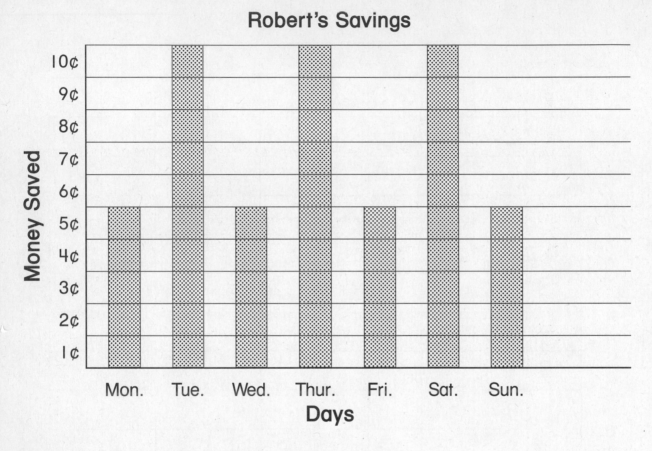

Robert's Savings

What pattern does the graph show? _____

_____

How much money did Robert save this week? _____

How much money would he save in 2 weeks if he followed

this exact pattern? _____

Notes for Home Your child recognized patterns of data in a graph and answered questions using information from the graph. *Home Activity:* Have your child challenge you with one more question related to the information in this graph.

Visual Thinking

Find your way from the dragon's cave.

Draw a blue line from the Cave to Home.

Pick up coins along the way.

There is more than one right answer.

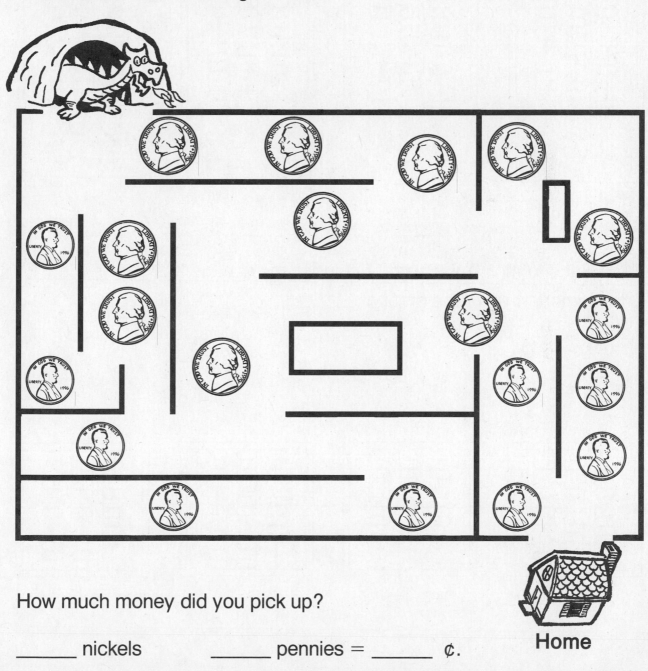

Home

How much money did you pick up?

_____ nickels   _____ pennies = _____ ¢.

Notes for Home Your child traced a path leading through a maze and "picked up" coins along the way. He or she then totaled the value of the coins. *Home Activity:* Ask your child to trace a different path through the maze using a different color crayon and then find the value of the new total of coins.

Name _____

Critical Thinking

An abacus can keep track of money. A shopkeeper
moves the beads to show what you pay. Tell what you pay.

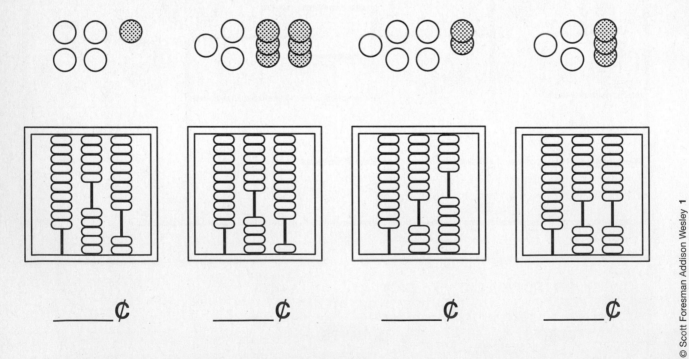

24¢   ____¢   ____¢   ____¢

Draw lines to match each set of coins to the abacus that shows the
same amount. Write the amount.

____¢   ____¢   ____¢   ____¢

© Scott Foresman Addison Wesley 1

Notes for Home Your child related sets of coins with abacuses and numerals showing the same amount.
Home Activity: Ask your child to use his or her fingers to show the number of cents in 3 dimes and 3 pennies. (33¢)

Name _____

Decision Making

You and two friends have earned some money.
You want to make equal groups of coins.

Draw a circle to show how many dimes each one of you gets.
Draw a circle to show how many pennies each one of you gets.

Use a different color crayon for each person.

How much money is left over? _____ ¢

What would you do with extra coins?
Draw a line under one of these ideas or write your own.

1. Buy a snack and share it.

2. Give the coins to help others.

3. Save the coins in your bank.

4. _____

Notes for Home Your child decided how to divide coins into 3 equal groups. Then he or she selected a way to use the extra money. *Home Activity:* Ask your child to separate sets of coins (such as 6 dimes and 7 pennies) into 3 equal groups, and to identify the value of the coins that are left. (For the example given, each group would have 2 dimes and 2 pennies. One penny would be left.)

Name _____

Decision Making

Find the value of each group of coins.

Circle the foods you would buy with that much money.

Write how much money is left after buying the items.

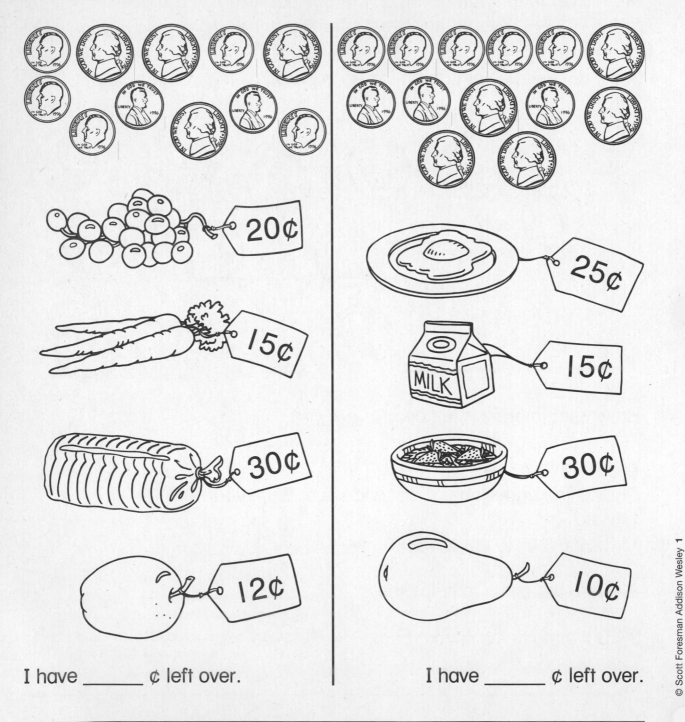

I have _____ ¢ left over.   I have _____ ¢ left over.

Notes for Home Your child counted groups of coins and then circled food items he or she would buy with that amount of money. *Home Activity:* Take your child to the grocery store to find out how much some of these items actually cost or look through a store advertisement for that information.

© Scott Foresman Addison Wesley 1

Name _____

Patterns in Data

Jerry helps his family sell fruit.

He uses these charts to tell how much things cost.

Fill in the missing numbers on the charts.

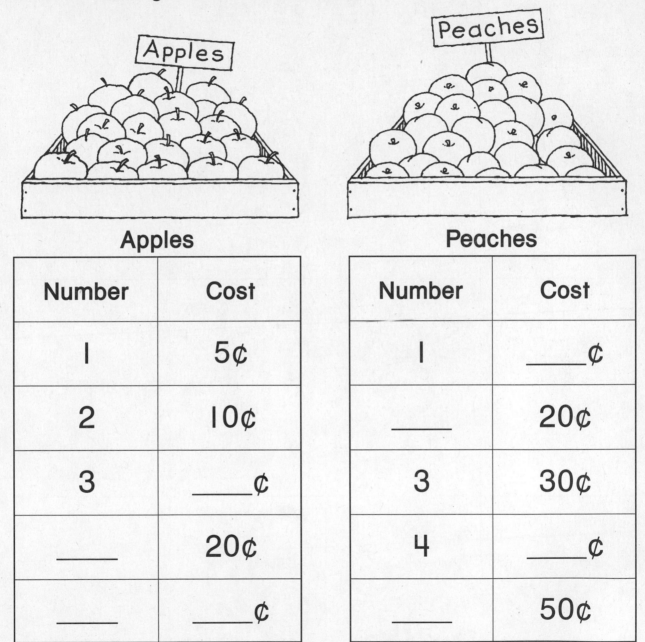

Apples

Number	Cost
1	5¢
2	10¢
3	____¢
____	20¢
____	____¢

Peaches

Number	Cost
1	____¢
____	20¢
3	30¢
4	____¢
____	50¢

In each chart, circle the most things you can buy with 1 quarter.

Notes for Home Your child recognized a pattern in price charts and filled in missing numbers. *Home Activity:* Ask your child to find the cost of 6 apples and 6 peaches. (30¢ and 60¢)

Name _____

Patterns in Numbers

Find the value of the coins. Write the amount on the line.
Draw the group of coins that comes next in each row.

You can draw (25¢), (10¢), (5¢), and (1¢).

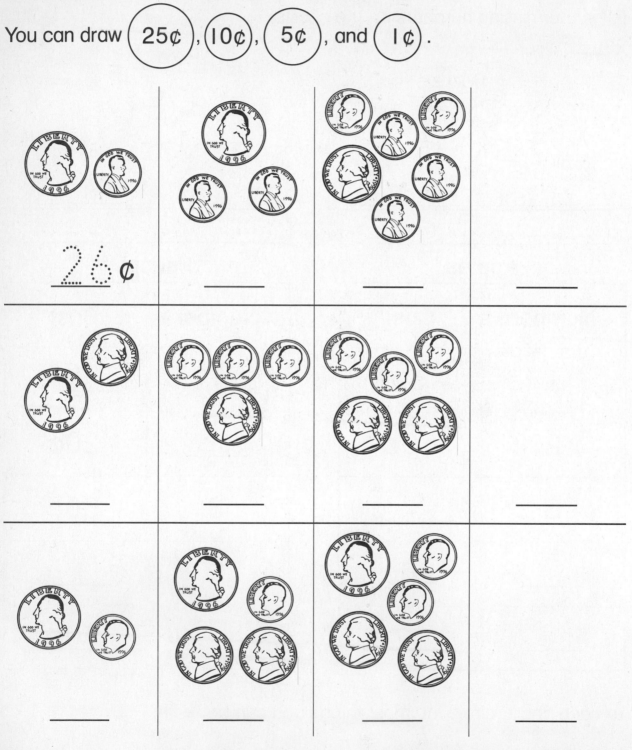

26¢

Notes for Home Your child found the value of groups of coins, identified a pattern based on their values, and selected the group of coins that would extend the pattern. *Home Activity:* Give your child a variety of coins and ask him or her to create an original pattern based on the amount the coins are worth.

Use with pages 347–348.

Name _____

Critical Thinking

Find the value of each set of coins.

Then cross out the set that is different.

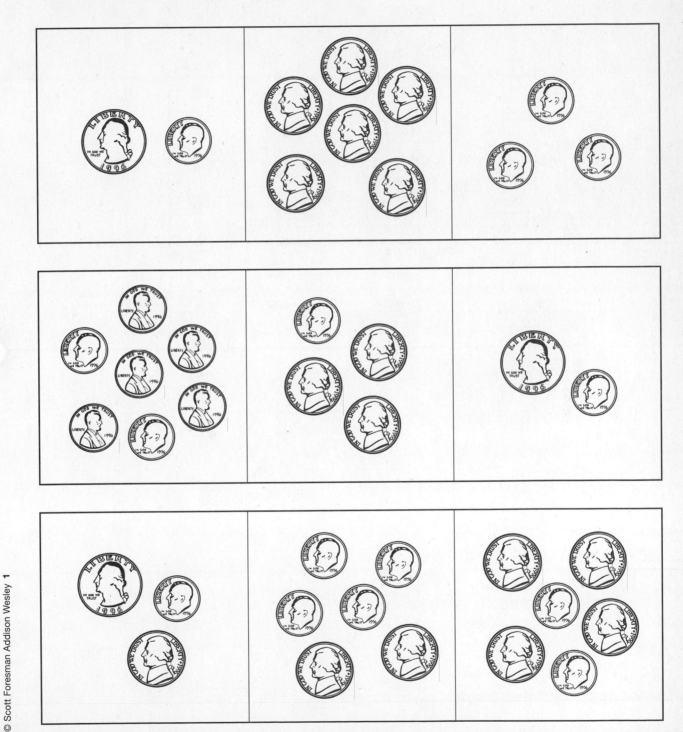

Notes for Home Your child found the set of coins in each row whose value was different. *Home Activity:* Ask your child to think of a third coin combination with the same value as the two matching sets in each row. (Answers may include: Row 1: 1 quarter, 1 nickel; Row 2: 3 dimes, 1 nickel; Row 3: 4 dimes.)

Name _____

Visual Thinking

Three friends had a sale.

This graph shows what they sold.

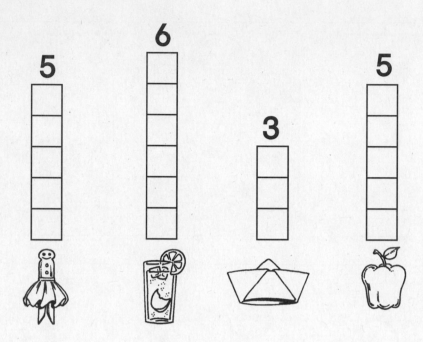

Which did the friends sell more of?

Which did they sell the most of?

How many things did they sell in all? _____

The friends wanted to earn more than 90¢.

If each thing cost [image of nickel], did they get their wish?   **Yes   No**

How much did the friends earn in all? _____

© Scott Foresman Addison Wesley 1

Notes for Home Your child read a graph about a sale and counted by 5s to find out how much money was earned. *Home Activity:* Ask your child to decide which of the items he or she would have bought at the sale and how much these items would have cost in all.

Name _____

Critical Thinking

Where could you find each tool for telling time?
Draw a line from a tool to a place.

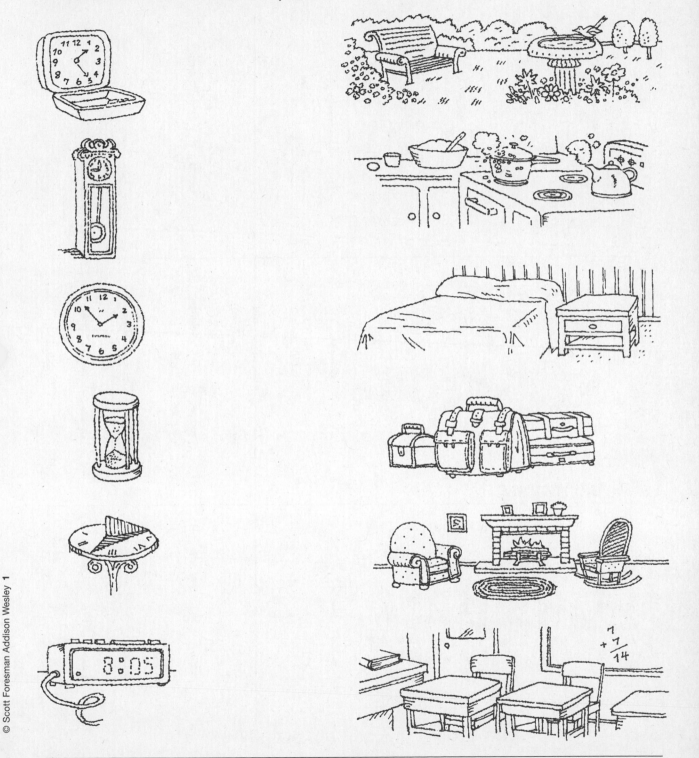

© Scott Foresman Addison Wesley 1

Notes for Home Your child matched clocks and other time-telling devices with scenes and activities with which they are useful. *Home Activity:* Ask your child to describe a situation when he or she needed to use a tool for telling time.

Name _____

Patterns in Time

Look for the pattern in each row.
Circle the clock that comes next.

Notes for Home Your child recognized and continued patterns which involved repeated addition of 2, 3, and 5 hours. *Home Activity:* Ask your child to show how he or she figured out the pattern in each row.

Visual Thinking

Connect the dot-to-dot times to find the
answer to this riddle:

What coat do you put on only when it is wet?

_____

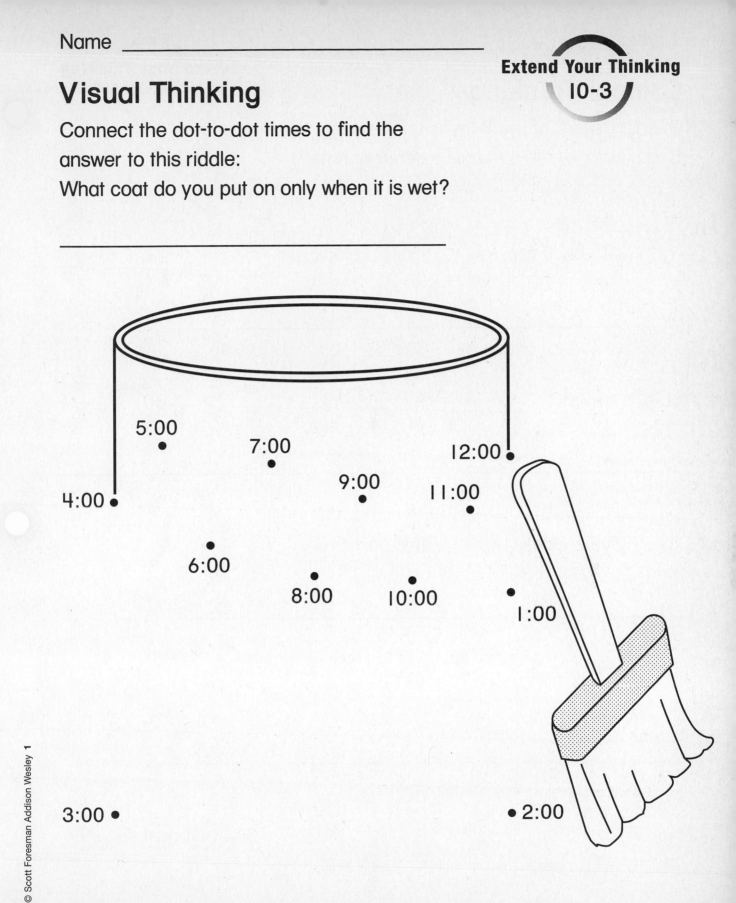

5:00

7:00

9:00

12:00

11:00

4:00

6:00

8:00   10:00

1:00

3:00   2:00

Notes for Home Your child connected digital times in correct order to solve a riddle.
Home Activity: Ask your child to read aloud each digital time.

Name _____

Critical Thinking

In each row, 2 of the 3 items tell the same time.
Cross out the one that tells a different time.

1. half past three   three o'clock

2. 7:00   7:30

3. five o'clock   half past five

4.   8:30   8 o'clock

5. 6:30   half past six

Notes for Home Your child compared the times shown 3 different ways, and then identified the one that was different. *Home Activity:* Ask your child to identify the time on the next half hour.

Name _____

Patterns in Data

Victor has many hobbies.

This is what he does each week.

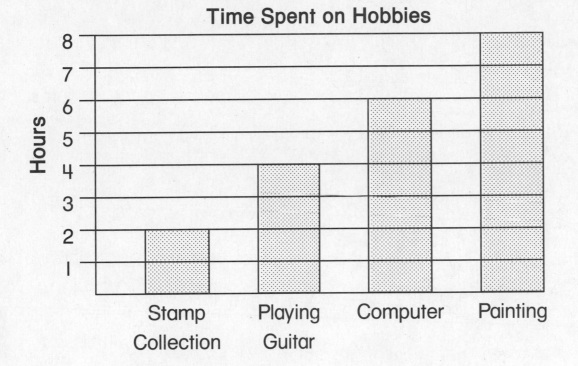

Time Spent on Hobbies

How much time does Victor spend on painting? _____

Does Victor spend more time on his computer or more time playing

his guitar? _____

How much longer? _____

How many hobbies does Victor have? _____

What pattern do you see on the graph? _____

_____

Notes for Home Your child used information from a graph to answer questions. *Home Activity:* Ask your child: *How many more hours does Victor spend painting than on his stamp collection?* (6 hours)

Name _____

Decision Making

How long would you spend doing each thing?

Tell how many hours and minutes each one would last.

Write the ending time.

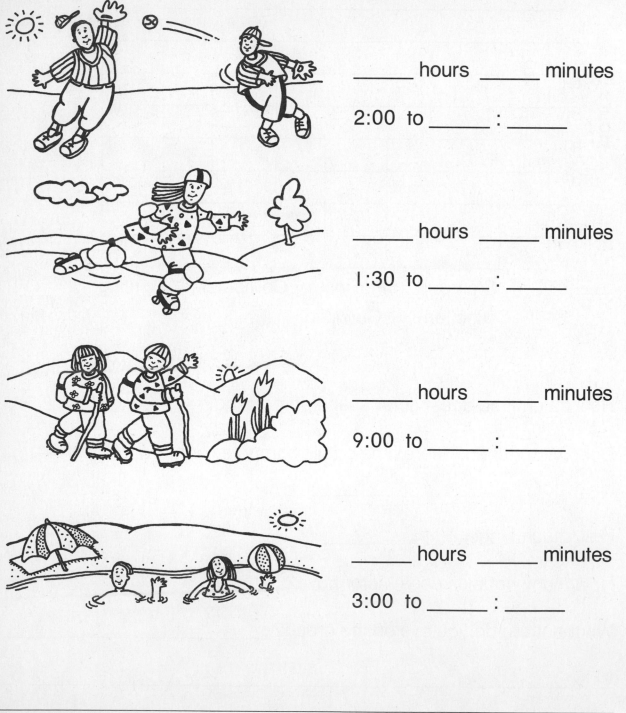

_____ hours _____ minutes

2:00 to _____ : _____

_____ hours _____ minutes

1:30 to _____ : _____

_____ hours _____ minutes

9:00 to _____ : _____

_____ hours _____ minutes

3:00 to _____ : _____

Notes for Home Your child decided how long he or she would like to spend for an activity and wrote the ending time in digital format. *Home Activity:* Ask your child to think of one more activity he or she enjoys doing and write the beginning and ending times for it.

Critical Thinking

Put the pictures in the correct order.

Write 1, 2, 3, or 4.

_____ _____ _____ _____

_____ _____ _____ _____

_____ _____ _____ _____

Notes for Home Your child sequenced each row of pictures in correct order by writing the number 1, 2, 3, or 4 below each picture. *Home Activity:* Ask your child to pantomime one of the activities in the correct order.

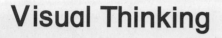

Visual Thinking

Play Tic-Tac-Time with a friend.

Try to be the first to draw times on clocks

that show the time in the correct order.

You can go from left to right, from top to bottom,

or from corner to corner.

Notes for Home Your child played a game drawing clocks that show the time in correct order. *Home Activity:* Ask your child to choose one row that was marked and figure out the time difference between the first and last clocks.

Name _____

Decision Making

Your summer camp offers these events
on certain days.
You may choose one for each day.
Write the letters of your choices on the
calendar for the week.

Event	Days
A Swim class	Sunday, Monday, Tuesday
B Walk in woods	Sunday, Tuesday, Thursday
C Baseball	Monday, Wednesday, Friday
D Make belt	Tuesday, Wednesday, Saturday
E Skating	Wednesday, Thursday, Friday
F Foot races	Thursday, Friday, Saturday
G Movie	Friday, Saturday

Weekly Calendar

Sunday	Monday	Tuesday	Wednesday	Thursday	Friday	Saturday

© Scott Foresman Addison Wesley 1

Notes for Home Your child selected activities scheduled for certain days and made up a personal schedule.
Home Activity: Keep a monthly calendar in the kitchen or other popular place in your home and encourage your
child to note on it his or her plans for specific days.

Name _____

Critical Thinking

Justin and Lisa made (·) to show how they

will spend time on Saturday.

Justin

do homework
clean room
watch TV
play baseball
play
help Dad
visit Tyrone
eat

Lisa

eat
visit Grandma
watch TV
clean room
practice piano
read
play

How many hours does Lisa spend

eating? _____   reading? _____   playing? _____

How many hours does Justin spend

playing baseball? _____   helping Dad? _____

Who looks at TV longer? _____   How much longer? _____

What does Justin spend 2 hours doing? _____

What does Justin spend the most time doing? _____

What does Lisa spend the most time doing? _____

Notes for Home Your child used clock faces to answer questions about time. *Home Activity:* Have your child trace one of the clocks on this page and show how he or she will spend time on Saturday.

Critical Thinking

How long is your hand?

If you think the animal or object is about 1 hand long, write I.

If you think the animal or object is shorter than your hand, write S.

If you think the animal or object is longer than your hand, write L.

_____   _____   _____   _____

_____   _____   _____   _____

_____   _____   _____   _____

© Scott Foresman Addison Wesley 1

Notes for Home Your child used his or her hand length to estimate the length of given objects as about 1 hand long, shorter than a hand, or longer than a hand. *Home Activity:* Ask your child to find one item in the home that is about the length of his or her hand, longer than his or her hand, and shorter than his or her hand.

Visual Thinking

People from Mars have landed.
Can you match each one with its name?
Write each name under the right picture.

1. Joe is 2 orgs tall.
    Aj is 4 orgs tall.
    Bu is only 1 org tall.
    Which is which?

    _____ _____ _____

2. Lqu is 2 orgs tall.
    Jun is 1 org tall.
    Ptz is 3 orgs tall.
    Which is which?

    _____ _____ _____

3. Zbr is the tallest.
    She is 5 orgs tall.
    The shortest is Ngt.
    About how tall is he?

    _____ orgs
    Fwi is a little taller.
    About how tall is he?

    _____ orgs

    _____ _____ _____

© Scott Foresman Addison Wesley 1

Notes for Home Your child used nonstandard units to compare and estimate lengths of creatures. *Home Activity:* Ask your child to think of a new unit of measure and name it. Then help him or her measure an object using the new, original unit of measure.

Visual Thinking

This shape has 12 arrows around it.

Count the arrows around each shape below.

Write the number of arrows inside the shape.

Color shapes with the same number of arrows the same color.

16 → blue   18 → red   20 → green

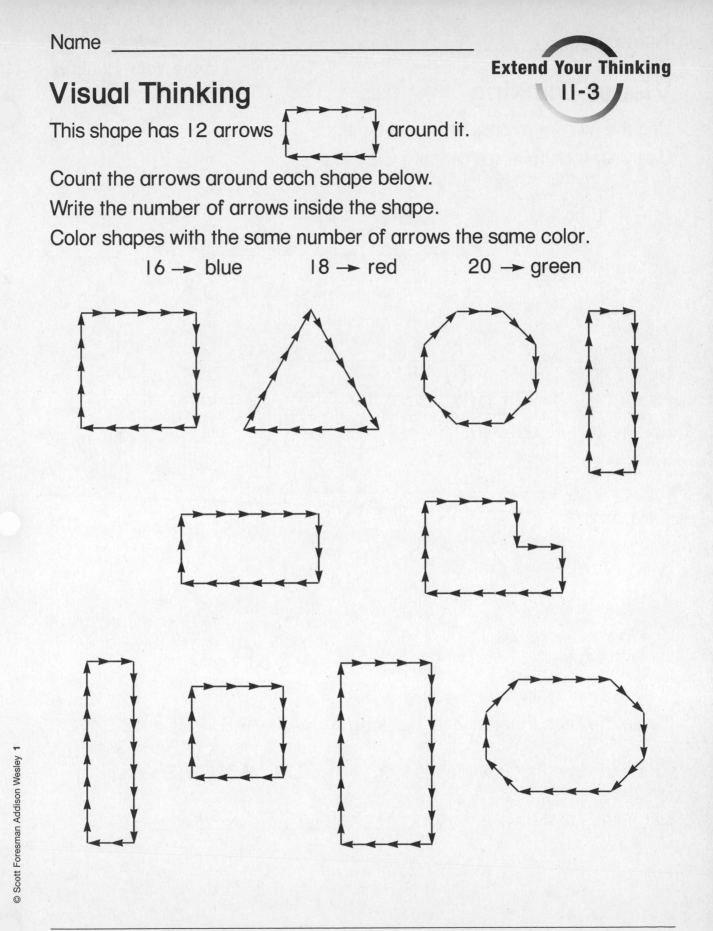

Notes for Home Your child used a nonstandard unit of measurement, the length of an arrow, to compare perimeters of several shapes. *Home Activity:* Ask your child to use a unit of measurement of his or her choice, such as a comb or spoon, to measure the distance around a radio or a television screen.

Name _____

Visual Thinking

Use the picture to answer each question.

Use your inch ruler to measure the lines.

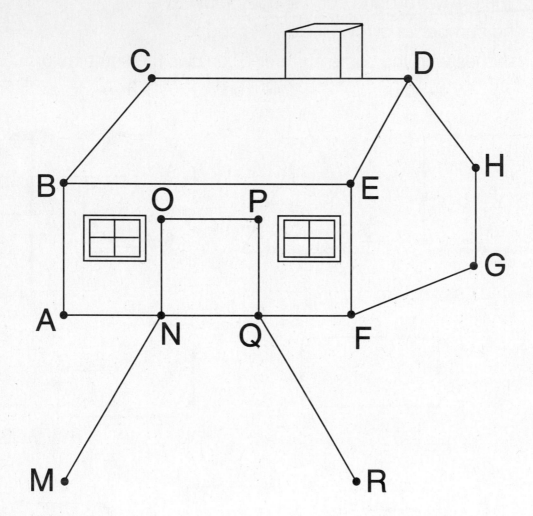

Circle the lines that are 3 inches long.   AF   AB   BC   BE   OP

Circle the line that is 2 inches long.   CD   MN   HG

List 4 lines that are 1 inch long. _____, _____, _____, _____.

Notes for Home Your child used an inch ruler to measure lines in a drawing and then compared line lengths.
Home Activity: Help your child use a ruler to measure the length of a book.

Name _____

Critical Thinking

Gina's doll is 8 centimeters tall.

Lucy's doll is 3 centimeters smaller than Gina's doll.

Magda's doll is 2 centimeters taller than Lucy's doll.

Anna's doll is 3 centimeters taller than Magda's doll.

Draw the dolls on the graph like this:

10 cm _____

9 cm _____

8 cm _____

7 cm _____

6 cm _____

5 cm _____

4 cm _____

3 cm _____

2 cm _____

1 cm _____

0 cm _____

    Gina's doll   Lucy's doll   Magda's doll   Anna's doll

Which doll is the tallest? _____ doll

Which doll is the smallest? _____ doll

How tall is Magda's doll? _____ centimeters

Notes for Home Your child found the height of dolls in centimeters compared to the height of other dolls and drew pictures of them. *Home Activity:* Ask your child to explain how he or she found the height of Anna's doll.

Name _____

Critical Thinking

Solve these problems.

1. Jumbo is 9 feet tall. Mumbo is 4 feet taller. How tall is Mumbo?

_____ feet

+ _____ feet
_____

_____ feet

2. The clown's stilts are 7 feet tall. If the clown sawed off 3 feet, how tall would the stilts be?

_____ feet

− _____ feet
_____

_____ feet

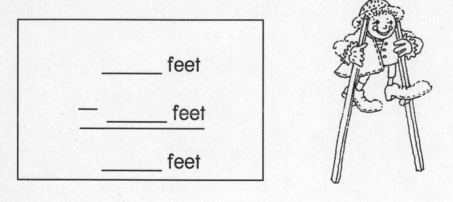

3. The high wire is 8 feet long. Carla wants to make it 4 feet longer. How long would it be then?

_____ feet

+ _____ feet
_____

_____ feet

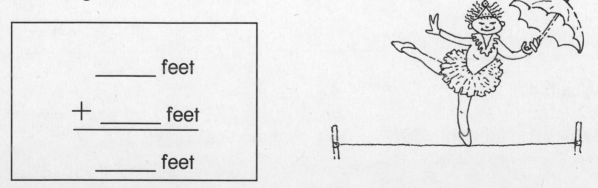

Notes for Home Your child solved addition and subtraction word problems involving lengths using feet.
Home Activity: Ask your child: *If the high wire was 2 feet shorter than 12 feet, how long would it be?*
(10 feet; 12 - 2 = 10)

Name _____

Decision Making

You and your friends go on a picnic.

Ugh! The table is very dirty and you forgot a tablecloth.

You can get one at a nearby shop.

Circle at least 2 things you can use to measure the table.

Put a red ✓ next to the one you think will work best.

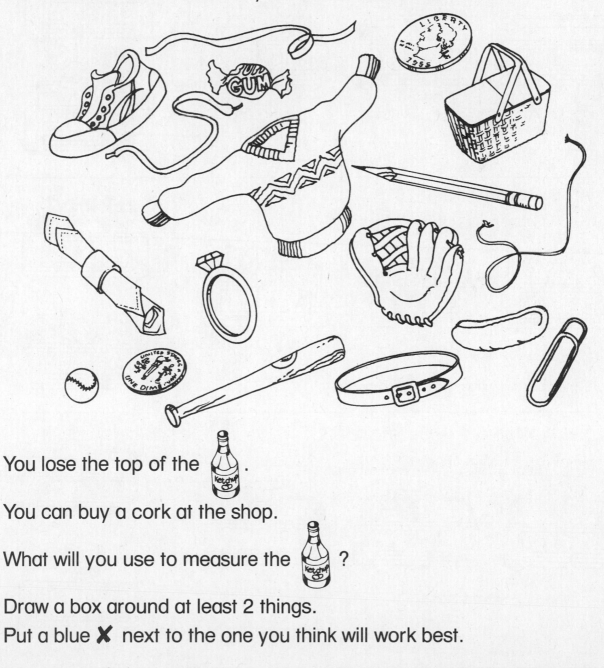

You lose the top of the .

You can buy a cork at the shop.

What will you use to measure the 🍾 ?

Draw a box around at least 2 things.

Put a blue ✗ next to the one you think will work best.

Notes for Home Your child selected objects that could be used to measure given objects. *Home Activity:* Ask your child to explain his or her choices.

Name _____

Patterns in Measurement

Read the scales. Find the pattern in each row.
Then circle the correct picture.

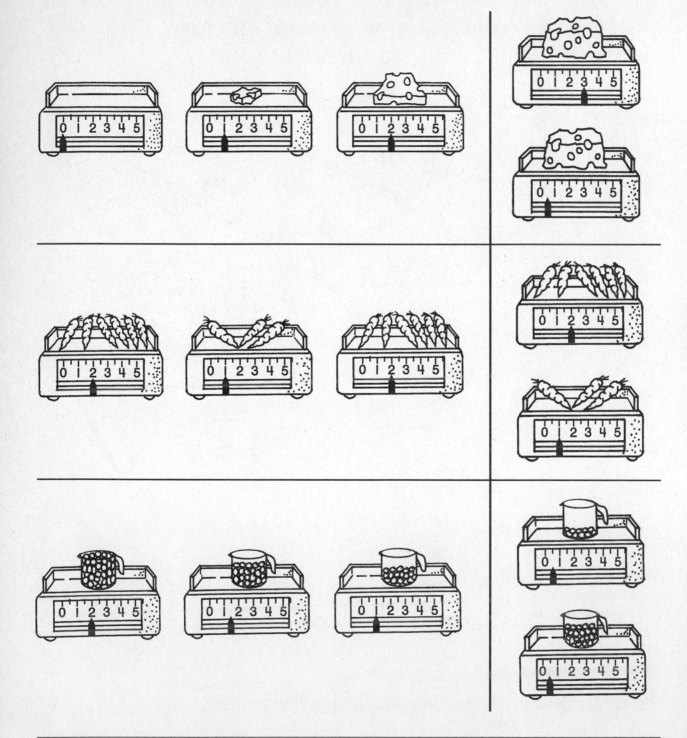

Notes for Home Your child identified a pattern in each row that involved comparing objects with regard to weight.
Home Activity: Have your child hold a 1-pound can of fruit or vegetables in one hand and hold another food, such as an orange, in the other hand and tell which is heavier.

Visual Thinking

Only animals that weigh 1 kilogram or less may
cross the bridge.

Circle each animal that may use the bridge.

Cross out the animals that are too heavy for the bridge.

© Scott Foresman Addison Wesley 1

Notes for Home Your child compared the weight of various animals and identified those weighing 1 kilogram or
less. *Home Activity:* Ask your child to find objects in your home that weigh 1 kilogram or less. (1 kilogram equals
about 2.2 pounds. Objects might include: crayon, pencil, tomato, etc.)

Name _____

Decision Making

Draw an X on the best answer.

1. You and a friend are thirsty. How much water
do you want?

2. You have 2 kittens. How much water do you
put in their water dish?

3. You have a plant that needs water. How much
do you give it?

4. You are making soup. How much water
will you add to the mix?

5. You want to wash an apple. How much
water do you need?

Notes for Home Your child decided whether a cup, a pint, or a quart of water should be used in various situations.
Home Activity: Ask your child to think of situations in which he or she uses a cup, a pint, and a quart of water.

Name _____

Critical Thinking

Solve each problem.

1. Jean needs to put a whole liter of water into a 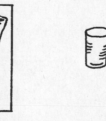.

   Which  should she use?

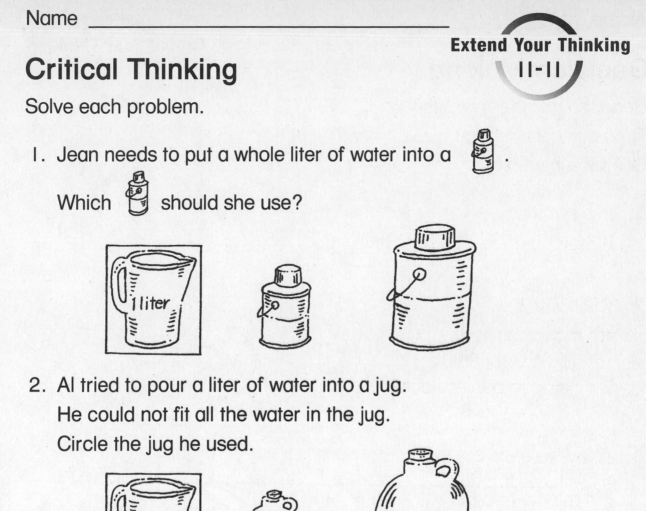

2. Al tried to pour a liter of water into a jug.
   He could not fit all the water in the jug.
   Circle the jug he used.

3. Su filled 4 glasses with a liter of water.
   Paul filled only 3 glasses with a liter of water.
   What size glass did Su use? What size glass did Paul use?
   Write the correct name under each glass.

_____   _____

Notes for Home Your child compared the capacity of pictured containers with that of liter containers.
Home Activity: Have your child fill a liter container—as from a soft drink—with water and then repeatedly pour the
water into a cup measure. Have him or her count the number of the cups the liter container fills up. (About 4 cups)

Decision Making

Read the weather reports.
Then decide what you would wear.
Color the pictures.

1. It is hot today.
   It may go up to 100°.

2. The snow is coming!
   It's going to be very cold.

3. It's raining and 58°.

4. A mild and sunny day is
   heading our way.
   It will go up to 75°.

5. It is a cold 32° today.
   Bundle up!

© Scott Foresman Addison Wesley 1

Notes for Home Your child decided what to wear based on given temperatures and weather reports.
Home Activity: Have your child listen with you to a weather report one morning, and then decide what he or she should wear for the day.

Name _____

Patterns in Data

Fill in the missing numbers in these charts.

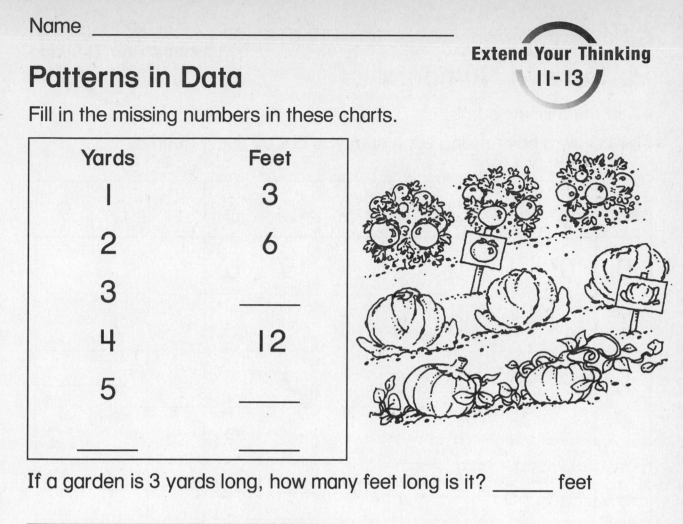

Yards	Feet
1	3
2	6
3	____
4	12
5	____
____	____

If a garden is 3 yards long, how many feet long is it? _____ feet

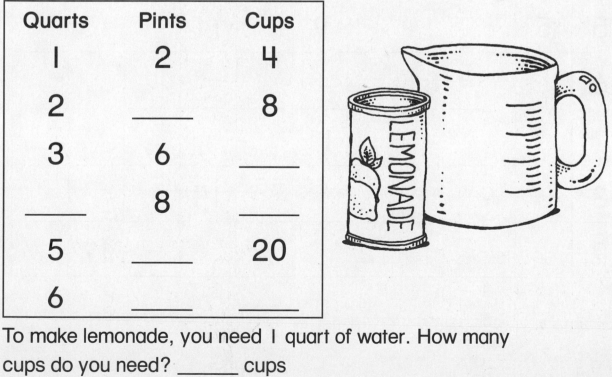

Quarts	Pints	Cups
1	2	4
2	____	8
3	6	____
____	8	____
5	____	20
6	____	____

To make lemonade, you need 1 quart of water. How many

cups do you need? _____ cups

Notes for Home Your child completed the patterns in charts converting yards to feet, and quarts to pints and cups. *Home Activity:* Ask your child to tell which is longer, 3 feet or 3 yards. (3 yards) Ask your child to tell which holds more liquid, 4 pints or 4 quarts. (4 quarts)

Patterns in Numbers

Fill in the missing sums.

Then draw a box around each sum you get by using doubles.

+	0	1	2	3	4	5	6	7	8	9
0	0	1	2	3	4	5	6			
1	1	2	3	4	5				9	
2	2	3	4	5		7				
3							9			12
4		5		7						
5	5				9		11		13	
6			8							
7					11					
8		9					14			
9			12						17	

© Scott Foresman Addison Wesley 1

Notes for Home Your child filled in the sums of facts through 18 and identified the sums produced by adding doubles, that is, by adding a number to itself. *Home Activity:* Ask your child to describe the design made by the boxed sums (a diagonal line) and the number pattern formed by the sums (counting by 2s).

Visual Thinking

Find your way out of the maze. Draw your path.

Follow the facts that use doubles and doubles plus one.

doubles fact	$3 + ? = 6$ $(3 + 3 = 6)$
double-plus-one	$3 + ? = 5$ and $3 + ? = 7$
other facts	$3 + ? = 4$ and $3 + ? = 8$ and more

$2 + ? = 10$	$9 + ? = 14$	$6 + ? = 9$	$7 + ? = 8$	$2 + ? = 8$
		$7 + ? = 10$		$8 + ? = 10$
$8 + ? = 13$	$8 + ? = 9$	$8 + ? = 16$	$6 + ? = 11$	$7 + ? = 16$
$3 + ? = 8$		$6 + ? = 12$	$5 + ? = 10$	
$3 + ? = 7$	$4 + ? = 8$	$4 + ? = 7$	$2 + ? = 5$	$4 + ? = 8$
$3 + ? = 5$		$5 + ? = 7$		$8 + ? = 15$
$3 + ? = 6$	$9 + ? = 15$	$6 + ? = 10$	$8 + ? = 12$	$9 + ? = 17$
START	$8 + ? = 11$		$2 + ? = 4$	$7 + ? = 14$
	$5 + ? = 13$	$9 + ? = 18$	$5 + ? = 11$	
		$7 + ? = 15$		
	$9 + ? = 12$	$2 + ? = 3$	$8 + ? = 17$	EXIT
	$4 + ? = 5$			

© Scott Foresman Addison Wesley 1

Notes for Home Your child identified facts that use doubles and doubles plus one, and then used the facts as a guide to find the path out of a maze. *Home Activity:* Ask your child to list all the doubles facts in the maze.
(8 + 8 = 16, 6 + 6 = 12, 5 + 5 = 10, 4 + 4 = 8, 3 + 3 = 6, 2 + 2 = 4, 7 + 7 = 14, 9 + 9 = 18)

Name _____

Critical Thinking

Choose one of these ways to solve the problems.

   Use a known fact.   Add doubles.   Make ten.

Two problems in each row can be solved in the same way.

In each row, cross out the problem that is different.

Then tell which way the two problems can be solved.

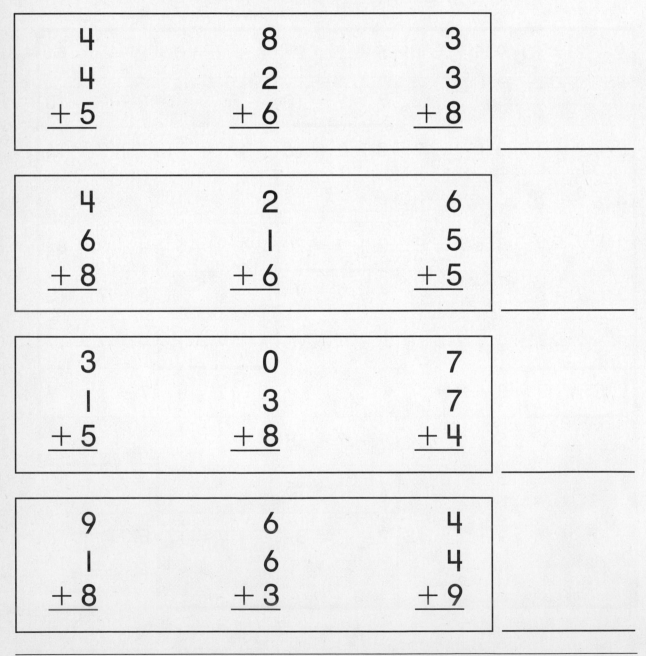

```
   4        8        3
   4        2        3
 + 5      + 6      + 8
_____  _____  _____     _____
```

```
   4        2        6
   6        1        5
 + 8      + 6      + 5
_____  _____  _____     _____
```

```
   3        0        7
   1        3        7
 + 5      + 8      + 4
_____  _____  _____     _____
```

```
   9        6        4
   1        6        4
 + 8      + 3      + 9
_____  _____  _____     _____
```

Notes for Home Given three 3-addend addition problems, your child identified two problems that can be solved by using the same strategy. *Home Activity:* Ask your child to identify the best strategy for solving each of the problems he or she crossed out. (Row 1: Make ten; Row 2: Use a known fact; Row 3: Add doubles; Row 4: Make ten.)

Critical Thinking

Fill in the missing number in each problem.

$$
\begin{array}{r}
1 \\
3 \\
+ \\
\hline
11
\end{array}
\qquad
\begin{array}{r}
7 \\
3 \\
+ \\
\hline
18
\end{array}
\qquad
\begin{array}{r}
4 \\
4 \\
+ \\
\hline
17
\end{array}
$$

$$
\begin{array}{r}
2 \\
1 \\
+ \\
\hline
10
\end{array}
\qquad
\begin{array}{r}
6 \\
4 \\
+ \\
\hline
16
\end{array}
\qquad
\begin{array}{r}
8 \\
8 \\
+ \\
\hline
18
\end{array}
$$

$$
\begin{array}{r}
3 \\
2 \\
+ \\
\hline
9
\end{array}
\qquad
\begin{array}{r}
9 \\
1 \\
+ \\
\hline
15
\end{array}
\qquad
\begin{array}{r}
6 \\
6 \\
+ \\
\hline
13
\end{array}
$$

Notes for Home Your child filled in the missing addends in addition problems involving 3 numbers, using these strategies—use facts you know, make ten, or add doubles. *Home Activity:* Ask your child to explain his or her reasoning to find one answer from each column.

Name _____

Patterns in Numbers

In each 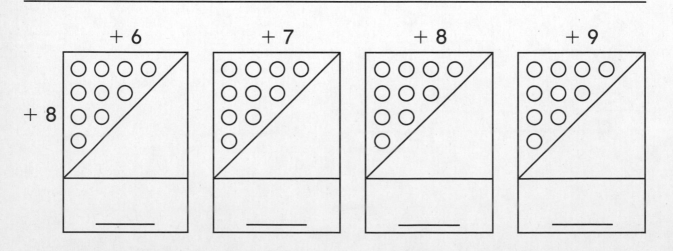, color dots to match the number at the left.

Then color as many more dots to match the number above.

If there are not enough dots, draw more dots in the ◿.

On the line, write the total number of colored dots.

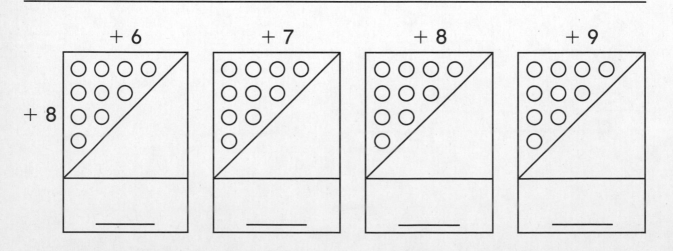

Notes for Home Your child used the make-10 strategy to illustrate the pattern formed by adding the numbers 2 through 5 to the numbers 8 and 9, and by adding the numbers 6 through 9 to the number 8. *Home Activity:* Ask your child to trace the four boxes in the last row and write the numeral 9 at the left. Then have him or her draw and count circles as in the exercise. (9 + 6 = 15; 9 + 7 = 16; 9 + 8 = 17; 9 + 9 = 18)

128 Use with pages 459–460.

Critical Thinking

Look at the numbers on this magic square.

Add from top to bottom, side to side, and corner to corner.

You will see that all the sums are 12.

7	0	5
2	4	6
3	8	1

The numbers in these magic squares also add up to 12.

Fill in the missing numbers.

3		7
	4	
		5

5		1
0	4	

Notes for Home Your child found the missing numbers in magic squares in which all the rows—vertically, horizontally, and diagonally—add up to 12. *Home Activity:* Ask your child to explain how he or she found the answers.

Visual Thinking

Draw lines to complete the picture.

Connect related addition and subtraction facts.

You may draw through other dots to connect related facts.

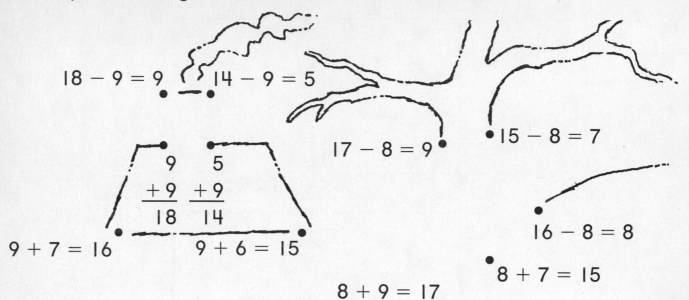

$18 - 9 = 9$ $14 - 9 = 5$

$17 - 8 = 9$ $15 - 8 = 7$

$\begin{array}{r} 9 \\ +9 \\ \hline 18 \end{array}$ $\begin{array}{r} 5 \\ +9 \\ \hline 14 \end{array}$

$9 + 7 = 16$ $9 + 6 = 15$ $16 - 8 = 8$

$8 + 7 = 15$

$8 + 9 = 17$

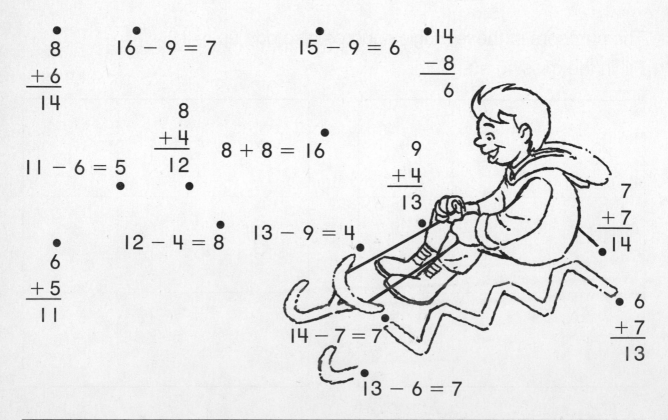

$\begin{array}{r} 8 \\ +6 \\ \hline 14 \end{array}$ $16 - 9 = 7$ $15 - 9 = 6$ $\begin{array}{r} 14 \\ -8 \\ \hline 6 \end{array}$

$\begin{array}{r} 8 \\ +4 \\ \hline 12 \end{array}$

$11 - 6 = 5$ $8 + 8 = 16$ $\begin{array}{r} 9 \\ +4 \\ \hline 13 \end{array}$ $\begin{array}{r} 7 \\ +7 \\ \hline 14 \end{array}$

$\begin{array}{r} 6 \\ +5 \\ \hline 11 \end{array}$ $12 - 4 = 8$ $13 - 9 = 4$ $\begin{array}{r} 6 \\ +7 \\ \hline 13 \end{array}$

$14 - 7 = 7$

$13 - 6 = 7$

Notes for Home Your child completed a dot-to-dot picture by drawing lines to connect related addition and subtraction facts through 18. *Home Activity:* Ask your child to state a related addition fact for each of these subtraction facts: 12 − 7 = 5 (7 + 5 = 12 or 5 + 7 = 12), 16 − 7 = 9 (7 + 9 = 16 or 9 + 7 = 16).

Critical Thinking

Match each word problem with an addition fact.
Then write the related subtraction fact.

$8 + 8 = 16$

1. A family of 14 whales lived in the sea. One day 7 swam away. How many whales are left now?

   The related subtraction fact is $14 - 7 = 7$.

   _____ whales are left.

$7 + 7 = 14$

2. There were 12 palm trees on the island. A big wind blew down 6 trees. How many trees are left?

   The related subtraction fact is _____.

   _____ trees are left.

$9 + 9 = 18$

3. 16 boats sailed to an island. Then, 8 boats sailed away. How many boats are left on the island?

   The related subtraction fact is _____.

   _____ boats are left.

$6 + 6 = 12$

4. Long ago, 18 ships sank in the sea. People have found 9 of them. How many ships are still lost?

   The related subtraction fact is _____.

   _____ ships are still lost.

Notes for Home Your child matched subtraction word problems with addition doubles facts that would help solve the problems and then wrote the related subtraction facts. *Home Activity:* Ask your child to change the numbers in one problem and to write both the addition and subtraction facts for that new problem.

Decision Making

Write the related subtraction fact for each fact in the box.

Choose one of the subtraction facts you wrote.

Use those numbers in a problem. Answer the problem.

Sample   __6__ birds were in a cage. __4__ flew away.

How many were left? __2__

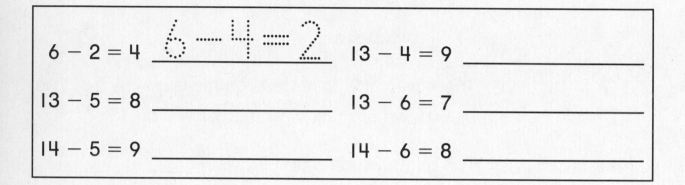

$6 - 2 = 4$ _6 — 4 = 2_ $13 - 4 = 9$ _____

$13 - 5 = 8$ _____ $13 - 6 = 7$ _____

$14 - 5 = 9$ _____ $14 - 6 = 8$ _____

1. Amy found _____ shells on the beach. _____ shells were pink.

   How many were not pink? _____

2. Juan lives _____ blocks from his grandfather. He starts to ride his

   bike to his grandfather's home. After _____ blocks he stops

   for a rest. How many more blocks must he go? _____

3. _____ sunflowers grew in the garden. During a storm,

   _____ sunflowers were blown down. How many were left
   standing? _____

© Scott Foresman Addison Wesley 1

Notes for Home Your child chose subtraction facts to use in story problems, identified their related subtraction facts, and completed the problems. *Home Activity:* Ask your child to tell you an original story problem that uses a subtraction fact related to one of the remaining facts in the box.

Visual Thinking

Each shape on the left flips to make a new shape.

A shape may flip side to side ⌐ ¬ or top to bottom ¬ ⌐.

Find the shape on the right that matches each shape on the left.

Inside, write the related subtraction fact.

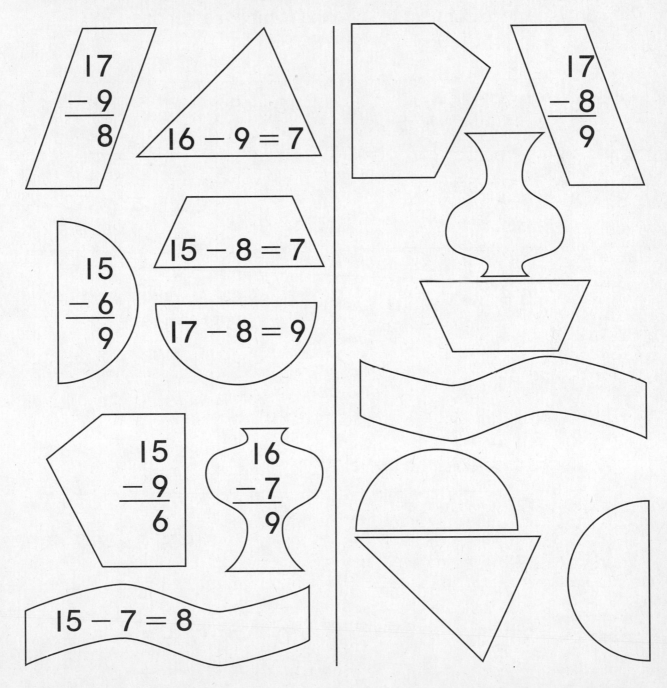

$$17 - 9 = 8$$

$$16 - 9 = 7$$

$$15 - 6 = 9$$

$$15 - 8 = 7$$

$$17 - 8 = 9$$

$$15 - 9 = 6$$

$$16 - 7 = 9$$

$$15 - 7 = 8$$

$$17 - 8 = 9$$

Notes for Home Your child matched shapes that were made by being flipped; then he or she wrote the related subtraction facts for 15 to 18 inside the new shapes. *Home Activity:* Ask your child to identify one more subtraction fact for 16 which has not been used on the left. (16 − 8 = 8)

Critical Thinking

Look at the Tic-Tac-Toe games below.

In each game, find two number sentences with the same sum or difference.

Write another number sentence with that answer to win.

Then draw a line to connect the winning number sentences.

6 + 6	4 + 9	
8 + 8	7 + 5	
7 + 6	5 + 9	

18 − 9		17 − 8
	14 − 6	
15 − 9		12 − 7

17 − 9	14 − 7	
	5 + 7	
6 + 2	9 + 6	13 − 8

12 − 5		
	14 − 8	8 − 4
13 − 7	7 + 3	5 + 9

© Scott Foresman Addison Wesley 1

Notes for Home Your child provided an addition or subtraction fact with the same answer as two others on each Tic-Tac-Toe board and drew a line connecting those facts. *Home Activity:* Ask your child to think of one other fact with the same answer as the one he or she provided above.

Decision Making

Choose a problem. Fill in the missing numbers.
Write the number sentence that solves your problem.

Use these numbers: 12   5   7.

_12_ boys were playing.   or   _____ boys were playing.

_5_ boys went home.   _____ boys joined them.

_7_ boys were left.   _____ boys were playing then.

_12 – 5 = 7_   _____

_____

Use these numbers: 15   9   6.

_____ dogs were in a show.   or   _____ dogs were in a show.

_____ dogs joined them.   _____ dogs were taken home.

_____ dogs were there in all.   _____ dogs were left.

_____   _____

Use these numbers: 16   9   7.

_____ flowers bloomed.   or   _____ flowers bloomed.

_____ flowers were sold.   _____ more flowers bloomed.

_____ flowers were left.   _____ flowers bloomed in all.

_____   _____

© Scott Foresman Addison Wesley 1

Notes for Home Your child chose an addition or a subtraction problem to solve. *Home Activity:* Ask your child to choose a problem he or she did not solve and solve it.

Name _____

Visual Thinking

Decide what number each arrow is hiding in
the hundred chart. Then add or subtract
the arrow's number from the hidden number.
Write each addition or subtraction sentence. Draw
a line from each arrow to its number sentence.

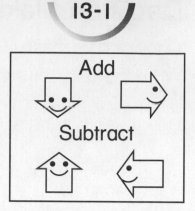

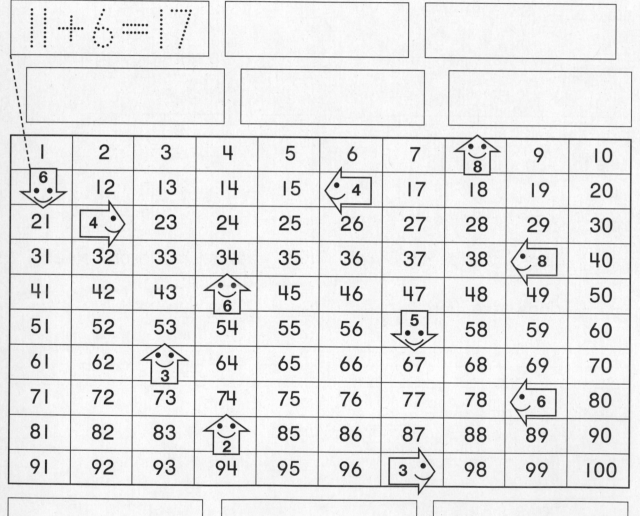

11 + 6 = 17

Notes for Home Your child wrote addition and subtraction number sentences related to a hundred chart.
Home Activity: Choose an addition problem and a subtraction problem. Have your child show you how he
or she can use the chart to solve each problem.

Decision Making

Each child spends 10 or 20 minutes doing an activity.

How many more minutes would you spend? Color the ⬭.

Then show the total time you would spend for each activity.

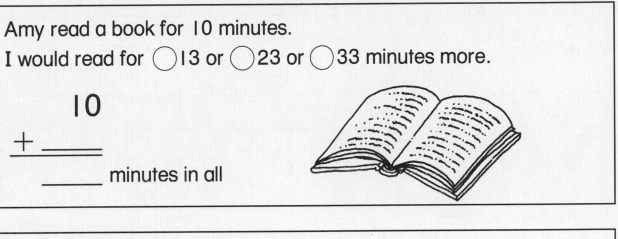

Amy read a book for 10 minutes.

I would read for ◯13 or ◯23 or ◯33 minutes more.

10
+ _____
_____ minutes in all

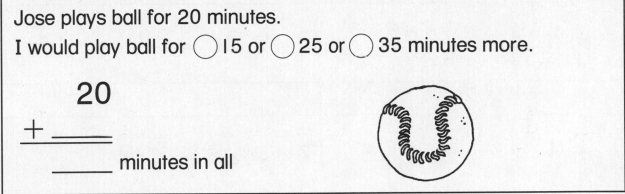

Jose plays ball for 20 minutes.

I would play ball for ◯15 or ◯25 or ◯35 minutes more.

20
+ _____
_____ minutes in all

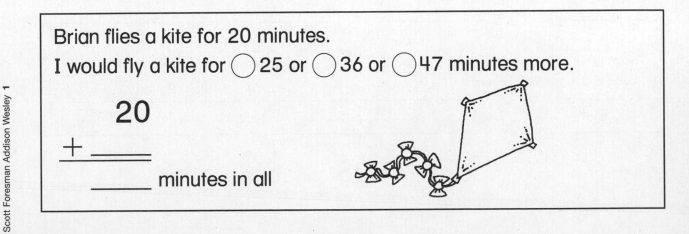

Brian flies a kite for 20 minutes.

I would fly a kite for ◯25 or ◯36 or ◯47 minutes more.

20
+ _____
_____ minutes in all

© Scott Foresman Addison Wesley 1

Notes for Home Your child chose how much more time he or she would like to spend doing different activities; then he or she added 2-digit numbers to 10 and 20 minutes. *Home Activity:* Ask your child how much longer than 10 minutes he or she would like to spend drawing a picture, and how many minutes that would be in all.

Name _____

Patterns in Numbers

Draw a line to match each pattern with a rule.

Then fill in the last number in each pattern.

Rule   Pattern

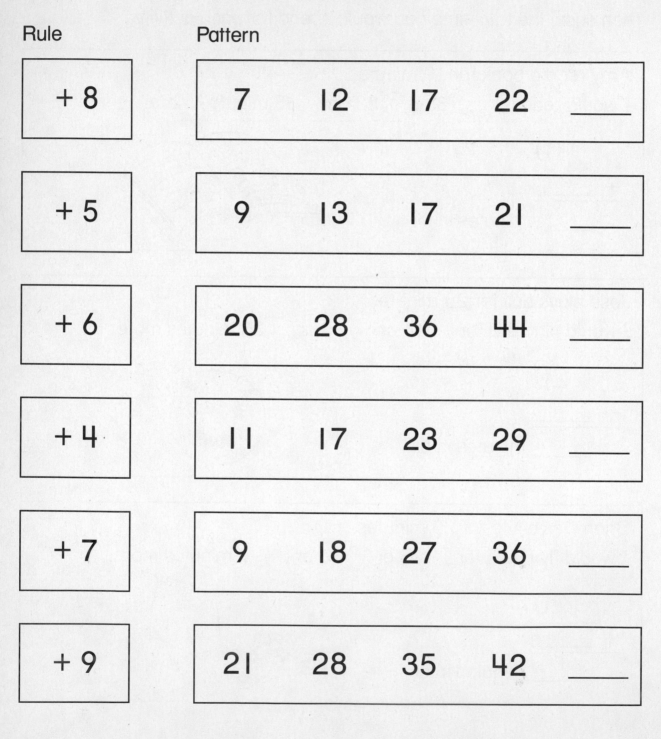

| +8 | 7   12   17   22   ___ |

| +5 | 9   13   17   21   ___ |

| +6 | 20   28   36   44   ___ |

| +4 | 11   17   23   29   ___ |

| +7 | 9   18   27   36   ___ |

| +9 | 21   28   35   42   ___ |

© Scott Foresman Addison Wesley 1

Notes for Home Your child identified rules for various number patterns involving adding 1-digit numbers to 2-digit numbers. *Home Activity:* Ask your child to explain how he or she found each rule.

Name _____

Critical Thinking

The sums for all the problems below are
given in the boxes at the right. First solve each problem.
Then write the matching letter for the sum on the line.
You will find answers to the riddles.

Sums
↓

The more you take away, the bigger it gets. What is it?

$$42 \quad\quad 15 \quad\quad 35 \quad\quad 23$$
$$+31 \quad\quad +82 \quad\quad +30 \quad\quad +35$$

E 58

H 73

A _____   _____   _____   _____

What starts with E, ends with E, and has 1 letter in it?

$$16 \quad\quad 33 \quad\quad 25 \quad\quad 31$$
$$+42 \quad\quad +13 \quad\quad +22 \quad\quad +27$$

L 65

N 46

AN _____   _____   _____   _____

$$55 \quad\quad 63 \quad\quad 20 \quad\quad 44$$
$$+10 \quad\quad +34 \quad\quad +61 \quad\quad +14$$

O 97

P 81

V 47

_____   _____   _____   _____

© Scott Foresman Addison Wesley 1

Notes for Home Your child added 2-digit numbers to find the answers to riddles. *Home Activity:* Ask your child to
make up problems whose sums spell another word, such as LOVE or HOPE.

Name _____

Patterns in Geometry

These are quilt squares.

A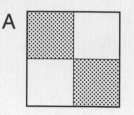

B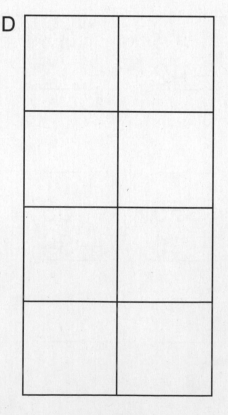

Look at Pattern A.

Draw Pattern A to make Pattern B.

How many times did you make

Pattern A in Pattern B? _____

C

D

Look at Pattern C.

Draw Pattern C to make Pattern D.

How many times did you make

Pattern C in Pattern D? _____

Notes for Home Your child identified the given patterns within larger patterns and predicted how the next stage of the pattern would look. *Home Activity:* Ask your child to draw his or her own quilt square that has a pattern.

Critical Thinking

These children were given secret numbers
by their teacher. They had to give clues so that
the class could guess the numbers.
Read the clues. Write each child's secret number.

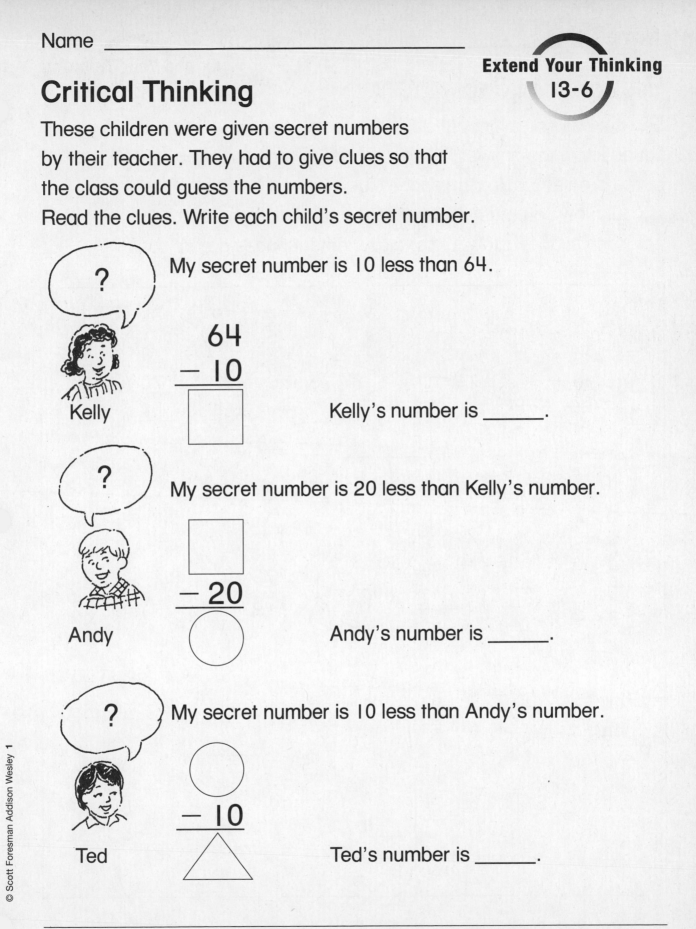

My secret number is 10 less than 64.

$$\begin{array}{r} 64 \\ -\ 10 \\ \hline \end{array}$$

Kelly

Kelly's number is _____.

My secret number is 20 less than Kelly's number.

$$\begin{array}{r} \\ -\ 20 \\ \hline \end{array}$$

Andy

Andy's number is _____.

My secret number is 10 less than Andy's number.

$$\begin{array}{r} \\ -\ 10 \\ \hline \end{array}$$

Ted

Ted's number is _____.

Notes for Home Your child solved a logical puzzle and subtracted 10 or a multiple of 10 from a 2-digit number.
Home Activity: Ask your child to find your secret number if it is 10 less than Ted's number. (14)

Visual Thinking

Look at each problem but do not write the answer.

If you know the answer is zero by just looking

at the problem, color the space blue.

If you know you must trade a ten for 10 ones to subtract,

color the shape yellow. Color all the other spaces green.

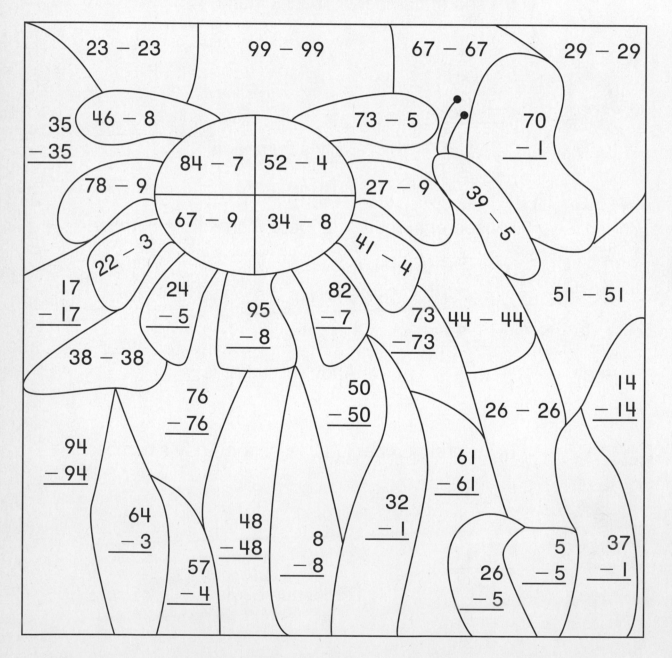

Notes for Home Your child identified subtraction problems that require replacing a ten with 10 ones, problems whose answers are zero, and other problems. *Home Activity:* Ask your child to tell you why a problem is colored yellow and then ask him or her to solve it.

Name _____

Critical Thinking

Read the problem.
Choose the way to solve it in the box.
Solve it and write the answer.

1. **54** children got on the bus.
13 got off at Main Street.
How many children were left
on the bus?

$$\begin{array}{ccc} 54 & 54 & 13 \\ +13 & -13 & -13 \end{array}$$

_____ children

2. **67** fans rooted for the home team.
56 fans rooted for the other team.
How many more fans rooted for the
home team?

$$\begin{array}{ccc} 67 & 56 & 67 \\ +0 & +67 & -56 \end{array}$$

_____ fans

3. **35** children worked in one garden.
12 children worked in another garden.
How many more children worked
in the first garden?

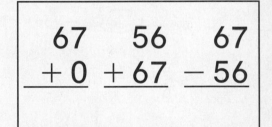

$$\begin{array}{ccc} 35 & 53 & 35 \\ -12 & -12 & +41 \end{array}$$

_____ children

© Scott Foresman Addison Wesley 1

Notes for Home Your child solved word problems by subtracting a 2-digit number from another 2-digit number.
Home Activity: Ask your child to make up a word problem about an event that happened today and then solve it.

Name _____

Decision Making

You are at a yard sale. You have 75¢.

Which things will you buy? Circle at least 4.

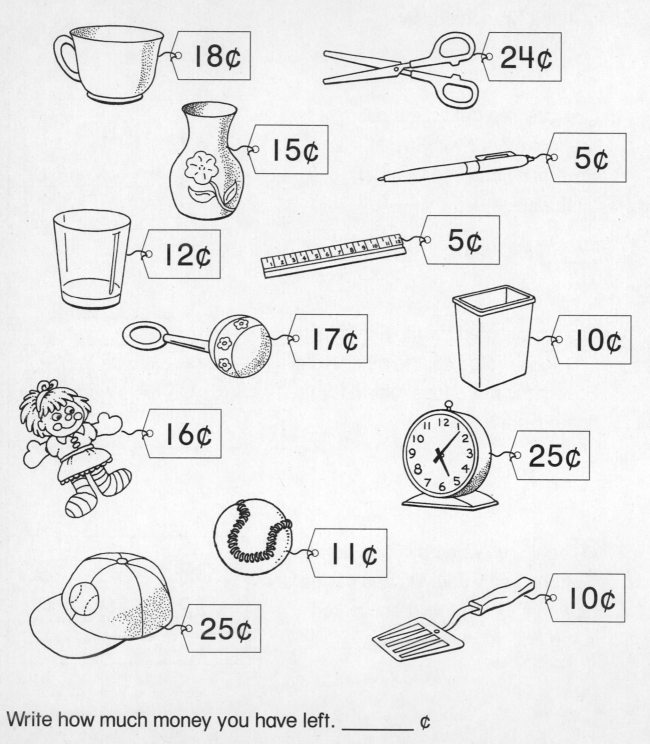

18¢

24¢

15¢

5¢

12¢

5¢

17¢

10¢

16¢

25¢

11¢

25¢

10¢

Write how much money you have left. _____ ¢

Notes for Home Your child used addition and/or subtraction of 1-digit and 2-digit numbers to select 4 items totaling no more than 75¢. *Home Activity:* Ask your child to tell how much more money he or she would need in order to buy, in addition to the circled things, a box of paints for 29¢.

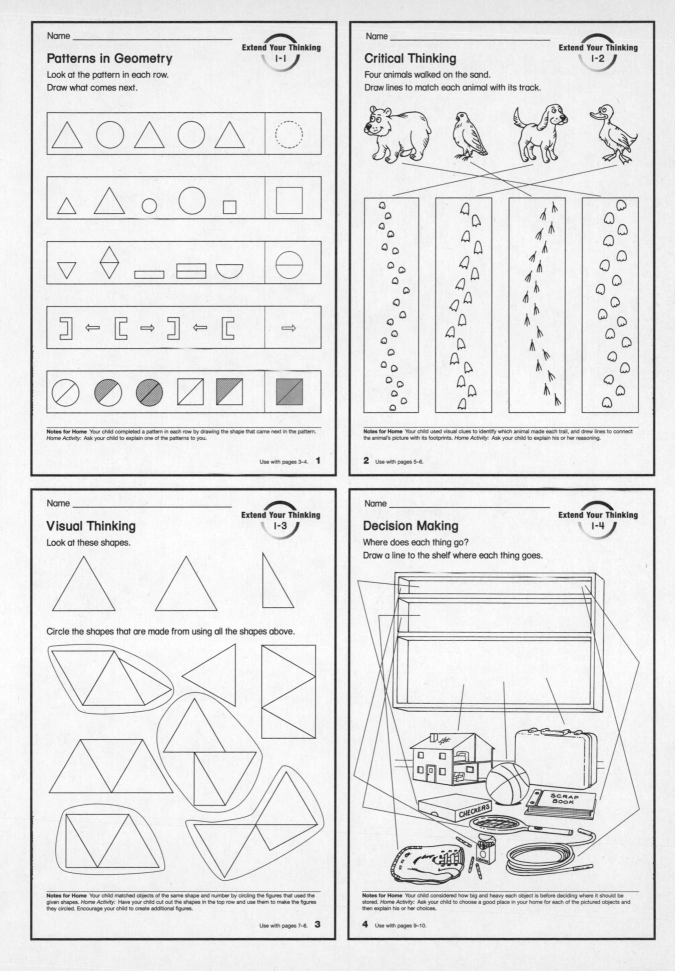

Name _____

Patterns in Geometry

Look at the pattern in each row.
Draw what comes next.

Notes for Home Your child completed a pattern in each row by drawing the shape that came next in the pattern.
Home Activity: Ask your child to explain one of the patterns to you.

Use with pages 3–4. **1**

Name _____

Critical Thinking

Four animals walked on the sand.
Draw lines to match each animal with its track.

Notes for Home Your child used visual clues to identify which animal made each trail, and drew lines to connect
the animal's picture with its footprints. *Home Activity:* Ask your child to explain his or her reasoning.

2 Use with pages 5–6.

Name _____

Visual Thinking

Look at these shapes.

Circle the shapes that are made from using all the shapes above.

Notes for Home Your child matched objects of the same shape and number by circling the figures that used the
given shapes. *Home Activity:* Have your child cut out the shapes in the top row and use them to make the figures
they circled. Encourage your child to create additional figures.

Use with pages 7–8. **3**

Name _____

Decision Making

Where does each thing go?
Draw a line to the shelf where each thing goes.

Notes for Home Your child considered how big and heavy each object is before deciding where it should be
stored. *Home Activity:* Ask your child to choose a good place in your home for each of the pictured objects and
then explain his or her choices.

4 Use with pages 9–10.

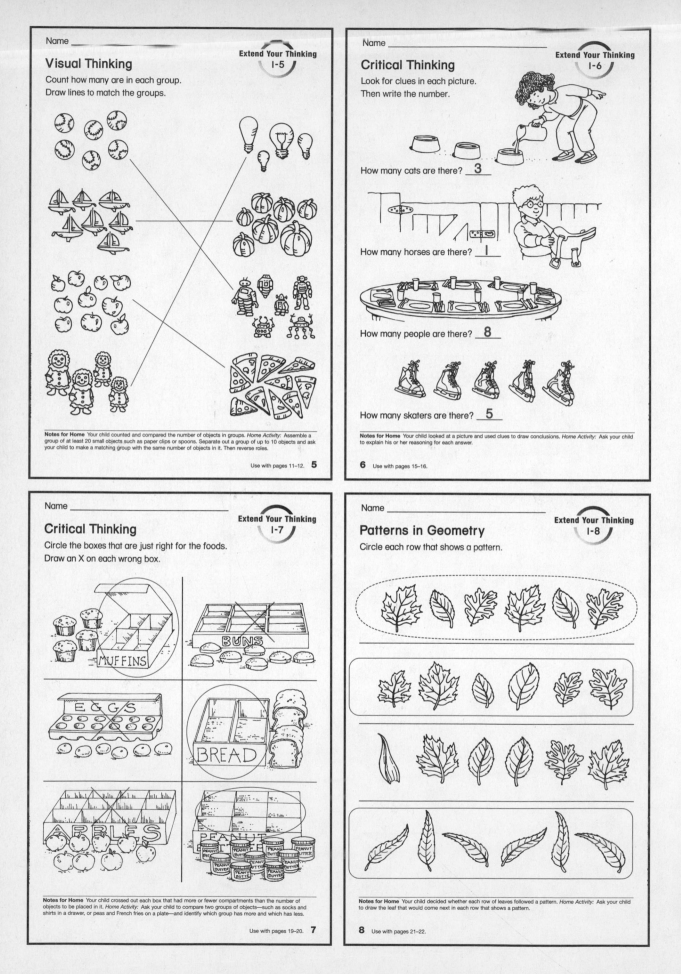

Visual Thinking

Count how many are in each group.
Draw lines to match the groups.

Notes for Home Your child counted and compared the number of objects in groups. *Home Activity:* Assemble a group of at least 20 small objects such as paper clips or spoons. Separate out a group of up to 10 objects and ask your child to make a matching group with the same number of objects in it. Then reverse roles.

Use with pages 11–12. **5**

Critical Thinking

Look for clues in each picture.
Then write the number.

How many cats are there? __3__

How many horses are there? __1__

How many people are there? __8__

How many skaters are there? __5__

Notes for Home Your child looked at a picture and used clues to draw conclusions. *Home Activity:* Ask your child to explain his or her reasoning for each answer.

6 Use with pages 15–16.

Critical Thinking

Circle the boxes that are just right for the foods.
Draw an X on each wrong box.

MUFFINS

BUNS

EGGS

BREAD

APPLES

PEANUT BUTTER

Notes for Home Your child crossed out each box that had more or fewer compartments than the number of objects to be placed in it. *Home Activity:* Ask your child to compare two groups of objects—such as socks and shirts in a drawer, or peas and French fries on a plate—and identify which group has more and which has less.

Use with pages 19–20. **7**

Patterns in Geometry

Circle each row that shows a pattern.

Notes for Home Your child decided whether each row of leaves followed a pattern. *Home Activity:* Ask your child to draw the leaf that would come next in each row that shows a pattern.

8 Use with pages 21–22.

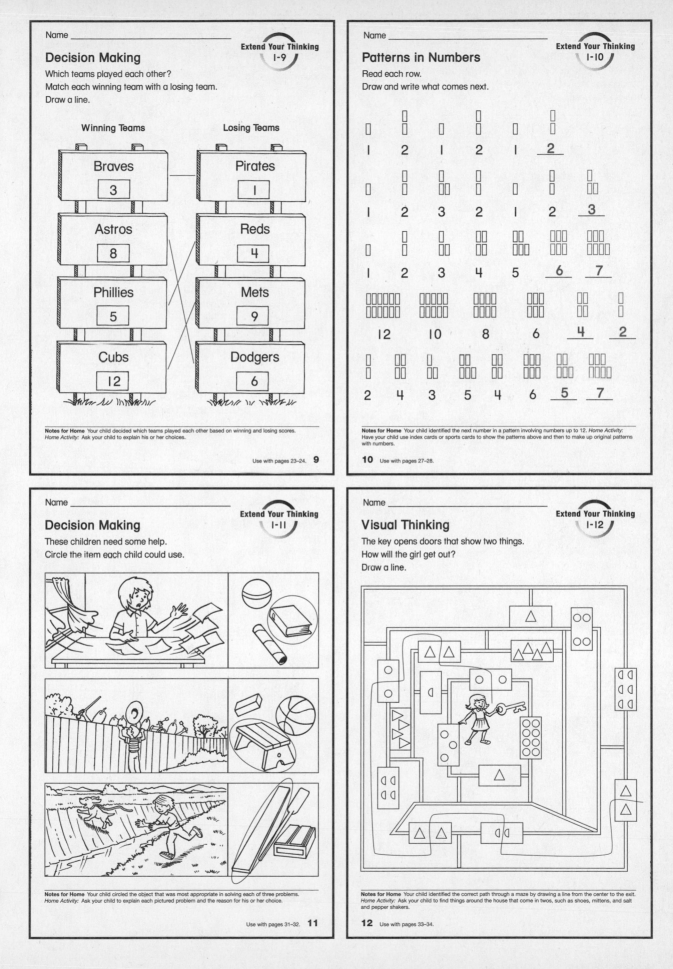

Name _____

Decision Making

Which teams played each other?
Match each winning team with a losing team.
Draw a line.

Winning Teams   Losing Teams

Braves   3   Pirates   1

Astros   8   Reds   4

Phillies   5   Mets   9

Cubs   12   Dodgers   6

Notes for Home Your child decided which teams played each other based on winning and losing scores.
Home Activity: Ask your child to explain his or her choices.

Use with pages 23–24. **9**

Name _____

Patterns in Numbers

Read each row.
Draw and write what comes next.

1 2 1 2 1 <u>2</u>

1 2 3 2 1 2 <u>3</u>

1 2 3 4 5 <u>6</u> <u>7</u>

12 10 8 6 <u>4</u> <u>2</u>

2 4 3 5 4 6 <u>5</u> <u>7</u>

Notes for Home Your child identified the next number in a pattern involving numbers up to 12. Home Activity: Have your child use index cards or sports cards to show the patterns above and then to make up original patterns with numbers.

10 Use with pages 27–28.

Name _____

Decision Making

These children need some help.
Circle the item each child could use.

Notes for Home Your child circled the object that was most appropriate in solving each of three problems.
Home Activity: Ask your child to explain each pictured problem and the reason for his or her choice.

Use with pages 31–32. **11**

Name _____

Visual Thinking

The key opens doors that show two things.
How will the girl get out?
Draw a line.

Notes for Home Your child identified the correct path through a maze by drawing a line from the center to the exit.
Home Activity: Ask your child to find things around the house that come in twos, such as shoes, mittens, and salt and pepper shakers.

12 Use with pages 33–34.

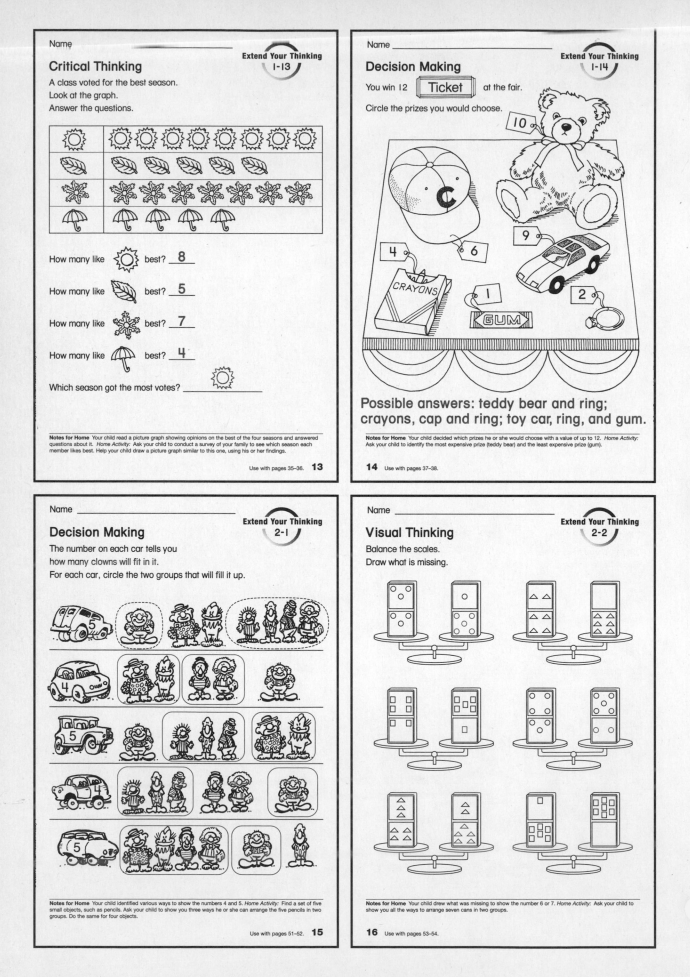

Critical Thinking

Extend Your Thinking 1-13

A class voted for the best season.
Look at the graph.
Answer the questions.

How many like ☀ best? __8__

How many like 🍃 best? __5__

How many like ❄ best? __7__

How many like ☂ best? __4__

Which season got the most votes? ☀

Notes for Home Your child read a picture graph showing opinions on the best of the four seasons and answered questions about it. *Home Activity:* Ask your child to conduct a survey of your family to see which season each member likes best. Help your child draw a picture graph similar to this one, using his or her findings.

Use with pages 35–36. **13**

Decision Making

Extend Your Thinking 1-14

You win 12 [Ticket] at the fair.

Circle the prizes you would choose.

Possible answers: teddy bear and ring; crayons, cap and ring; toy car, ring, and gum.

Notes for Home Your child decided which prizes he or she would choose with a value of up to 12. *Home Activity:* Ask your child to identify the most expensive prize (teddy bear) and the least expensive prize (gum).

14 Use with pages 37–38.

Decision Making

Extend Your Thinking 2-1

The number on each car tells you
how many clowns will fit in it.
For each car, circle the two groups that will fill it up.

Notes for Home Your child identified various ways to show the numbers 4 and 5. *Home Activity:* Find a set of five small objects, such as pencils. Ask your child to show you three ways he or she can arrange the five pencils in two groups. Do the same for four objects.

Use with pages 51–52. **15**

Visual Thinking

Extend Your Thinking 2-2

Balance the scales.
Draw what is missing.

Notes for Home Your child drew what was missing to show the number 6 or 7. *Home Activity:* Ask your child to show you all the ways to arrange seven cans in two groups.

16 Use with pages 53–54.

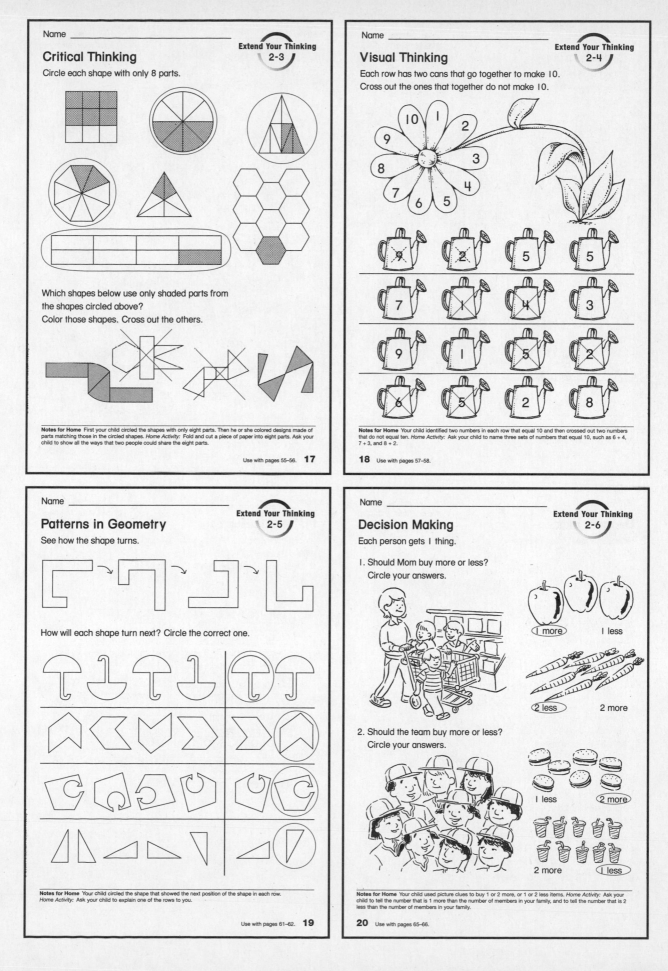

Critical Thinking

Circle each shape with only 8 parts.

Which shapes below use only shaded parts from the shapes circled above?
Color those shapes. Cross out the others.

Notes for Home First your child circled the shapes with only eight parts. Then he or she colored designs made of parts matching those in the circled shapes. *Home Activity:* Fold and cut a piece of paper into eight parts. Ask your child to show all the ways that two people could share the eight parts.

Use with pages 55–56. **17**

Visual Thinking

Each row has two cans that go together to make 10.
Cross out the ones that together do not make 10.

Notes for Home Your child identified two numbers in each row that equal 10 and then crossed out two numbers that do not equal ten. *Home Activity:* Ask your child to name three sets of numbers that equal 10, such as 6 + 4, 7 + 3, and 8 + 2.

18 Use with pages 57–58.

Patterns in Geometry

See how the shape turns.

How will each shape turn next? Circle the correct one.

Notes for Home Your child circled the shape that showed the next position of the shape in each row. *Home Activity:* Ask your child to explain one of the rows to you.

Use with pages 61–62. **19**

Decision Making

Each person gets 1 thing.

1. Should Mom buy more or less?
   Circle your answers.

   1 more   1 less

   2 less   2 more

2. Should the team buy more or less?
   Circle your answers.

   1 less   2 more

   2 more   1 less

Notes for Home Your child used picture clues to buy 1 or 2 more, or 1 or 2 less items. *Home Activity:* Ask your child to tell the number that is 1 more than the number of members in your family, and to tell the number that is 2 less than the number of members in your family.

20 Use with pages 65–66.

149

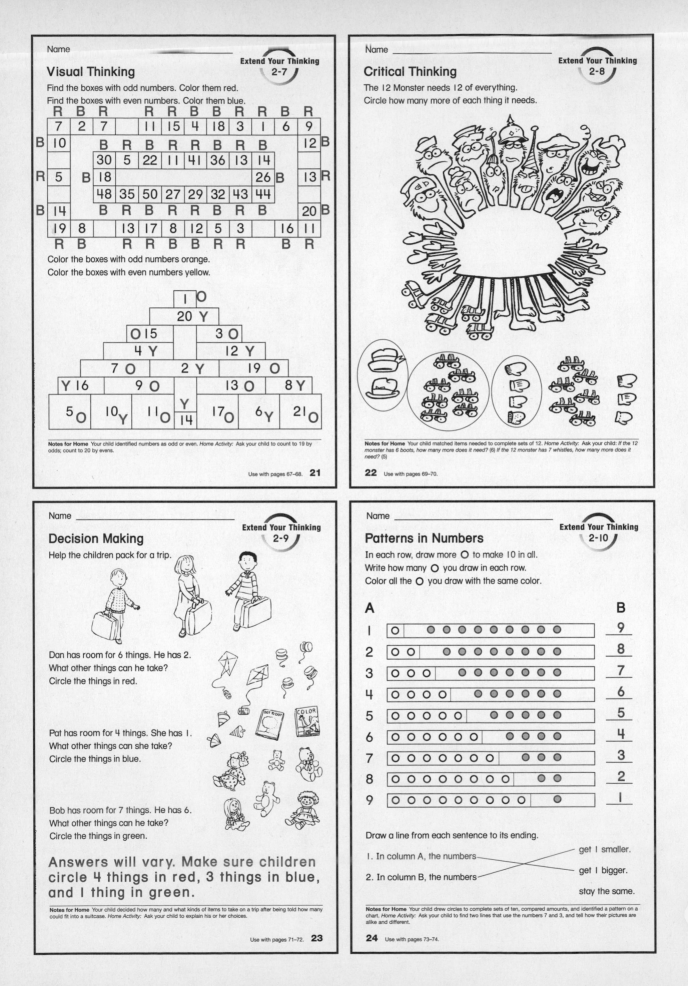

Visual Thinking

Find the boxes with odd numbers. Color them red.
Find the boxes with even numbers. Color them blue.

	R	B	R		R	R	B	B	R		R	B	R
	7	2	7		11	15	4	18	3	1	6	9	
B	10		B	R	B	R	R	B	R	B		12	B
		30	5	22	11	41	36	13	14		
R	5	B	18					26	B	13	R
		48	35	50	27	29	32	43	44		
B	14		B	R	B	R	R	B	R	B		20	B
	19	8		13	17	8	12	5	3		16	11	
	R	B		R	R	B	B	R	R		B	R	

Color the boxes with odd numbers orange.
Color the boxes with even numbers yellow.

```
              1 O
             20 Y
        O 15      3 O
         4 Y      12 Y
      7 O     2 Y     19 O
   Y 16    9 O     13 O    8 Y
  5 O  10 Y  11 O   Y    17 O  6 Y  21 O
                    14
```

Notes for Home Your child identified numbers as odd or even. *Home Activity:* Ask your child to count to 19 by odds; count to 20 by evens.

Critical Thinking

The 12 Monster needs 12 of everything.
Circle how many more of each thing it needs.

Notes for Home Your child matched items needed to complete sets of 12. *Home Activity:* Ask your child: *If the 12 monster has 6 boots, how many more does it need?* (6) *If the 12 monster has 7 whistles, how many more does it need?* (5)

Decision Making

Help the children pack for a trip.

Dan has room for 6 things. He has 2.
What other things can he take?
Circle the things in red.

Pat has room for 4 things. She has 1.
What other things can she take?
Circle the things in blue.

Bob has room for 7 things. He has 6.
What other things can he take?
Circle the things in green.

Answers will vary. Make sure children circle 4 things in red, 3 things in blue, and 1 thing in green.

Notes for Home Your child decided how many and what kinds of items to take on a trip after being told how many could fit into a suitcase. *Home Activity:* Ask your child to explain his or her choices.

Patterns in Numbers

In each row, draw more ○ to make 10 in all.
Write how many ○ you draw in each row.
Color all the ○ you draw with the same color.

A		B
1	○ ● ● ● ● ● ● ● ● ●	9
2	○ ○ ● ● ● ● ● ● ● ●	8
3	○ ○ ○ ● ● ● ● ● ● ●	7
4	○ ○ ○ ○ ● ● ● ● ● ●	6
5	○ ○ ○ ○ ○ ● ● ● ● ●	5
6	○ ○ ○ ○ ○ ○ ● ● ● ●	4
7	○ ○ ○ ○ ○ ○ ○ ● ● ●	3
8	○ ○ ○ ○ ○ ○ ○ ○ ● ●	2
9	○ ○ ○ ○ ○ ○ ○ ○ ○ ●	1

Draw a line from each sentence to its ending.

1. In column A, the numbers ——— get 1 smaller.

2. In column B, the numbers ——— get 1 bigger.

stay the same.

Notes for Home Your child drew circles to complete sets of ten, compared amounts, and identified a pattern on a chart. *Home Activity:* Ask your child to find two lines that use the numbers 7 and 3, and tell how their pictures are alike and different.

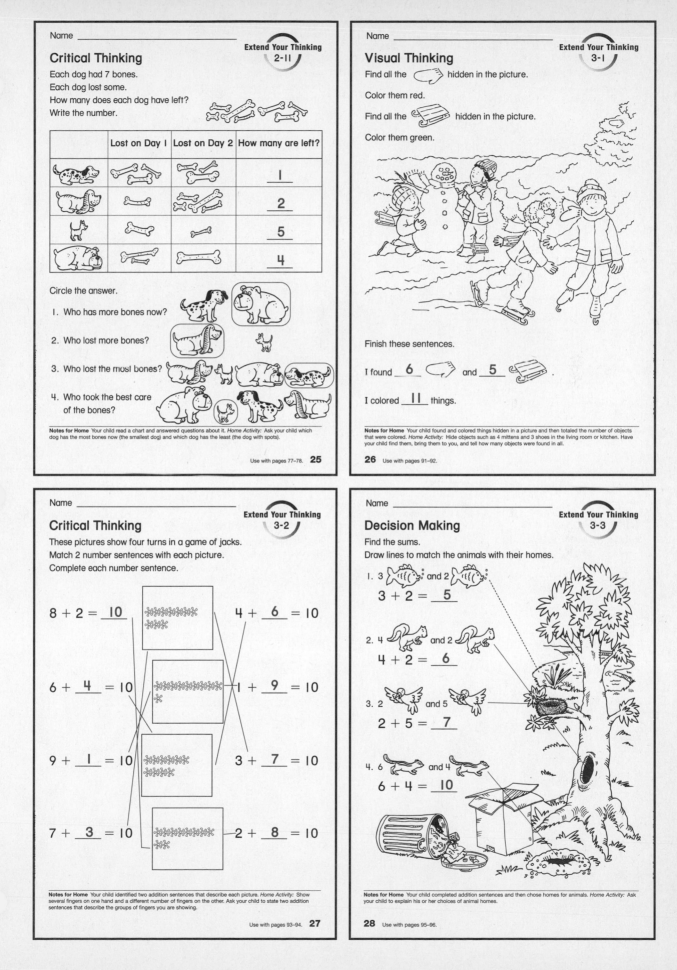

Name _____

Critical Thinking

Each dog had 7 bones.
Each dog lost some.
How many does each dog have left?
Write the number.

	Lost on Day 1	Lost on Day 2	How many are left?
			1
			2
			5
			4

Circle the answer.

1. Who has more bones now?

2. Who lost more bones?

3. Who lost the most bones?

4. Who took the best care of the bones?

Notes for Home Your child read a chart and answered questions about it. *Home Activity:* Ask your child which dog has the most bones now (the smallest dog) and which dog has the least (the dog with spots).

Use with pages 77–78. **25**

Name _____

Visual Thinking

Find all the ⊙ hidden in the picture.

Color them red.

Find all the ⬭ hidden in the picture.

Color them green.

Finish these sentences.

I found __6__ 🧤 and __5__ 🛷 .

I colored __11__ things.

Notes for Home Your child found and colored things hidden in a picture and then totaled the number of objects that were colored. *Home Activity:* Hide objects such as 4 mittens and 3 shoes in the living room or kitchen. Have your child find them, bring them to you, and tell how many objects were found in all.

26 Use with pages 91–92.

Name _____

Critical Thinking

These pictures show four turns in a game of jacks.
Match 2 number sentences with each picture.
Complete each number sentence.

$8 + 2 = \underline{10}$ $4 + \underline{6} = 10$

$6 + \underline{4} = 10$ $1 + \underline{9} = 10$

$9 + \underline{1} = 10$ $3 + \underline{7} = 10$

$7 + \underline{3} = 10$ $2 + \underline{8} = 10$

Notes for Home Your child identified two addition sentences that describe each picture. *Home Activity:* Show several fingers on one hand and a different number of fingers on the other. Ask your child to state two addition sentences that describe the groups of fingers you are showing.

Use with pages 93–94. **27**

Name _____

Decision Making

Find the sums.
Draw lines to match the animals with their homes.

1. 3 🐟 and 2 🐟
   $3 + 2 = \underline{5}$

2. 4 🐿 and 2 🐿
   $4 + 2 = \underline{6}$

3. 2 🐦 and 5 🐦
   $2 + 5 = \underline{7}$

4. 6 🐿 and 4 🐿
   $6 + 4 = \underline{10}$

Notes for Home Your child completed addition sentences and then chose homes for animals. *Home Activity:* Ask your child to explain his or her choices of animal homes.

28 Use with pages 95–96.

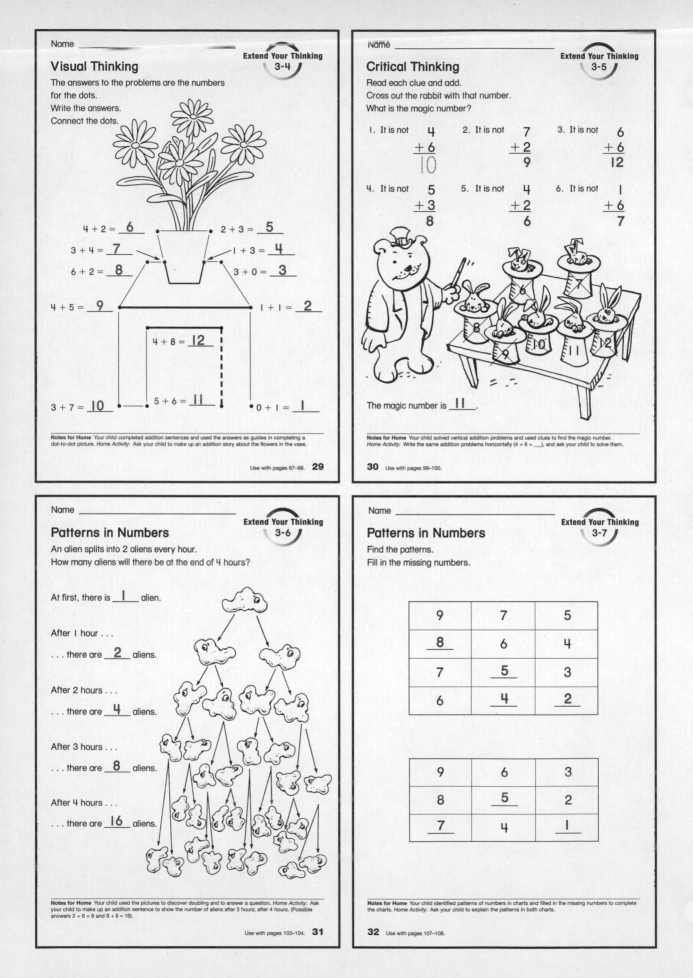

Visual Thinking

The answers to the problems are the numbers for the dots.
Write the answers.
Connect the dots.

4 + 2 = __6__   2 + 3 = __5__

3 + 4 = __7__   1 + 3 = __4__

6 + 2 = __8__   3 + 0 = __3__

4 + 5 = __9__   1 + 1 = __2__

4 + 8 = __12__

3 + 7 = __10__   5 + 6 = __11__   0 + 1 = __1__

Notes for Home Your child completed addition sentences and used the answers as guides in completing a dot-to-dot picture. *Home Activity:* Ask your child to make up an addition story about the flowers in the vase.

Use with pages 97–98. **29**

Critical Thinking

Read each clue and add.
Cross out the rabbit with that number.
What is the magic number?

1. It is not
$$\begin{array}{r} 4 \\ + 6 \\ \hline 10 \end{array}$$

2. It is not
$$\begin{array}{r} 7 \\ + 2 \\ \hline 9 \end{array}$$

3. It is not
$$\begin{array}{r} 6 \\ + 6 \\ \hline 12 \end{array}$$

4. It is not
$$\begin{array}{r} 5 \\ + 3 \\ \hline 8 \end{array}$$

5. It is not
$$\begin{array}{r} 4 \\ + 2 \\ \hline 6 \end{array}$$

6. It is not
$$\begin{array}{r} 1 \\ + 6 \\ \hline 7 \end{array}$$

The magic number is __11__.

Notes for Home Your child solved vertical addition problems and used clues to find the magic number. *Home Activity:* Write the same addition problems horizontally (4 + 6 = ___), and ask your child to solve them.

30 Use with pages 99–100.

Patterns in Numbers

An alien splits into 2 aliens every hour.
How many aliens will there be at the end of 4 hours?

At first, there is __1__ alien.

After 1 hour . . .

. . . there are __2__ aliens.

After 2 hours . . .

. . . there are __4__ aliens.

After 3 hours . . .

. . . there are __8__ aliens.

After 4 hours . . .

. . . there are __16__ aliens.

Notes for Home Your child used the pictures to discover doubling and to answer a question. *Home Activity:* Ask your child to make up an addition sentence to show the number of aliens after 3 hours; after 4 hours. (Possible answers 2 + 6 = 8 and 8 + 8 = 16).

Use with pages 103–104. **31**

Patterns in Numbers

Find the patterns.
Fill in the missing numbers.

9	7	5
8	6	4
7	5	3
6	4	2

9	6	3
8	5	2
7	4	1

Notes for Home Your child identified patterns of numbers in charts and filled in the missing numbers to complete the charts. *Home Activity:* Ask your child to explain the patterns in both charts.

32 Use with pages 107–108.

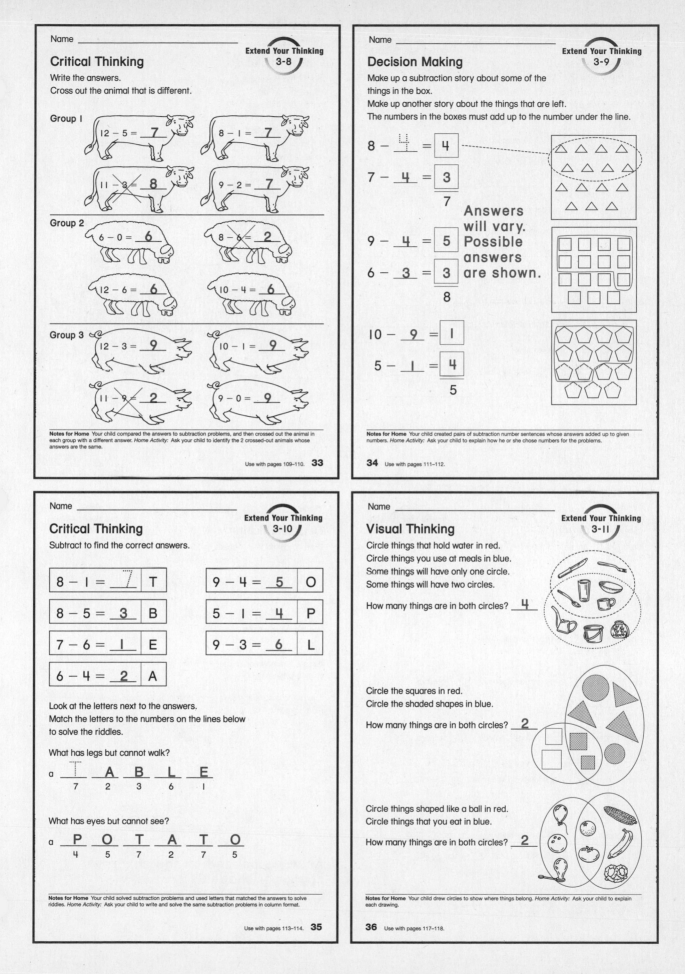

Name _____

Critical Thinking

Write the answers.
Cross out the animal that is different.

Group 1

12 − 5 = _7_

8 − 1 = _7_

11 − 3 = _8_

9 − 2 = _7_

Group 2

6 − 0 = _6_

8 − 6 = _2_

12 − 6 = _6_

10 − 4 = _6_

Group 3

12 − 3 = _9_

10 − 1 = _9_

11 − 9 = _2_

9 − 0 = _9_

Notes for Home Your child compared the answers to subtraction problems, and then crossed out the animal in each group with a different answer. *Home Activity:* Ask your child to identify the 2 crossed-out animals whose answers are the same.

Use with pages 109–110. **33**

Name _____

Decision Making

Make up a subtraction story about some of the things in the box.
Make up another story about the things that are left.
The numbers in the boxes must add up to the number under the line.

8 − _4_ = [4]

7 − _4_ = [3]

_7_

9 − _4_ = [5]

6 − _3_ = [3]

_8_

Answers will vary. Possible answers are shown.

10 − _9_ = [1]

5 − _1_ = [4]

_5_

Notes for Home Your child created pairs of subtraction number sentences whose answers added up to given numbers. *Home Activity:* Ask your child to explain how he or she chose numbers for the problems.

34 Use with pages 111–112.

Name _____

Critical Thinking

Subtract to find the correct answers.

8 − 1 = _7_	T
8 − 5 = _3_	B
7 − 6 = _1_	E
6 − 4 = _2_	A

9 − 4 = _5_	O
5 − 1 = _4_	P
9 − 3 = _6_	L

Look at the letters next to the answers.
Match the letters to the numbers on the lines below to solve the riddles.

What has legs but cannot walk?

a _T_ _A_ _B_ _L_ _E_
   7   2   3   6   1

What has eyes but cannot see?

a _P_ _O_ _T_ _A_ _T_ _O_
   4   5   7   2   7   5

Notes for Home Your child solved subtraction problems and used letters that matched the answers to solve riddles. *Home Activity:* Ask your child to write and solve the same subtraction problems in column format.

Use with pages 113–114. **35**

Name _____

Visual Thinking

Circle things that hold water in red.
Circle things you use at meals in blue.
Some things will have only one circle.
Some things will have two circles.

How many things are in both circles? _4_

Circle the squares in red.
Circle the shaded shapes in blue.

How many things are in both circles? _2_

Circle things shaped like a ball in red.
Circle things that you eat in blue.

How many things are in both circles? _2_

Notes for Home Your child drew circles to show where things belong. *Home Activity:* Ask your child to explain each drawing.

36 Use with pages 117–118.

Decision Making

Read the problem.
Write + or − and the answer.
Write what the children can do.

10 children are at a party. 2 children leave.

$10 - 2 = 8$ What can they play? _____

_____

2 girls are outside. 1 girl comes over.

$2 + 1 = 1$ What can they play? _____

_____

6 children are camping. 2 children go home.

$6 - 2 = 4$ What can they do? _____

_____

1 boy has a ball. 1 boy joins him.

$1 + 1 = 2$ What can they play? _____

_____

Notes for Home Your child completed number sentences to match given situations, then described an activity that the children in the situation could enjoy. Home Activity: Ask your child to make up a situation like the ones on this page. Have him or her write a number sentence to match the story.

Visual Thinking

Play with a classmate. Take turns trying to get
from Start to End.
For each turn, toss a coin.
If it lands heads up, move 1 space by coloring 1 square
on your game board.
If it lands tails up, move 2 spaces by coloring two squares
on your game board.
Count as you jump. See who gets to the End first.

Notes for Home Your child counted on to find sums through 12. Home Activity: Ask your child how much is 4 and 3. (7)

Critical Thinking

Complete the sentence for each child.

Jack: I have _6_ cars and Jill has _5_ cars. $6 + 5 = 11$

Jill: I have _5_ cars and Jack has _6_ cars. $5 + 6 = 11$

Rosa: I have _7_ brushes and Beth has _5_ brushes.
$7 + 5 = 12$

Beth: I have _5_ brushes and Rosa has _7_ brushes.
$5 + 7 = 12$

Mimi: I have _3_ balloons and Don has _7_ balloons.
$3 + 7 = 10$

Don: I have _7_ 7 balloons and Mimi has _3_ 3 balloons.
$7 + 3 = 10$

Luc: I have _9_ dogs and Sam has _3_ dogs. $9 + 3 = 12$

Sam: I have _3_ dogs and Luc has _9_ dogs. $3 + 9 = 12$

Notes for Home Your child wrote two different addition facts to describe the same number of objects. Home Activity: Divide 11 spoons between you and your child and have your child make up two different addition sentences with the facts 8 and 3. (8 + 3 = 11; 3 + 8 = 11) Repeat with a different division of the spoons.

Decision Making

Draw an animal with 2 heads and 3 legs.
Choose one of these shapes for the body.

Use a different shape for the 2 heads.
Use the last shape for the 3 legs.

Write 1 in each body shape.
Write 2 in each head shape.
Write 3 in each leg shape.

Then write a number from your animal in each shape below.
Find the sums.

7   5   6   8   9

6   9   8   7   7

Answers depend on the children's choice of shapes.

Notes for Home Your child found sums by adding 1, 2, or 3 to greater addends. Home Activity: Ask your child to find the sums of 9 + 3 (12), 8 + 3 (11), 6 + 3 (9), 9 + 2 (11), and 7 + 2 (9).

Patterns in Numbers

Draw what comes next in each pattern.
Show the pattern on the number line.
Write + 1, + 2, or + 3 on the line to the right.

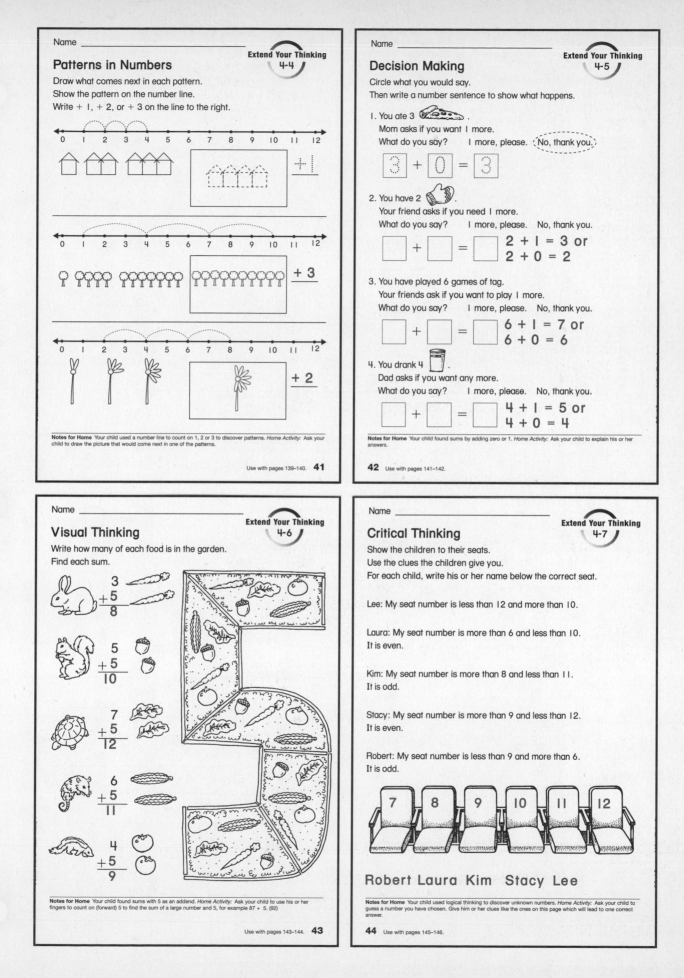

0 1 2 3 4 5 6 7 8 9 10 11 12

+ 1

0 1 2 3 4 5 6 7 8 9 10 11 12

+ 3

0 1 2 3 4 5 6 7 8 9 10 11 12

+ 2

Notes for Home Your child used a number line to count on 1, 2 or 3 to discover patterns. *Home Activity:* Ask your child to draw the picture that would come next in one of the patterns.

Use with pages 139–140. **41**

Decision Making

Circle what you would say.
Then write a number sentence to show what happens.

1. You ate 3 🍕 .
   Mom asks if you want 1 more.
   What do you say?   1 more, please.   (No, thank you.)

   $3 + 0 = 3$

2. You have 2 🧤 .
   Your friend asks if you need 1 more.
   What do you say?   1 more, please.   No, thank you.

   ☐ + ☐ = ☐   2 + 1 = 3 or
                  2 + 0 = 2

3. You have played 6 games of tag.
   Your friends ask if you want to play 1 more.
   What do you say?   1 more, please.   No, thank you.

   ☐ + ☐ = ☐   6 + 1 = 7 or
                  6 + 0 = 6

4. You drank 4 🥤 .
   Dad asks if you want any more.
   What do you say?   1 more, please.   No, thank you.

   ☐ + ☐ = ☐   4 + 1 = 5 or
                  4 + 0 = 4

Notes for Home Your child found sums by adding zero or 1. *Home Activity:* Ask your child to explain his or her answers.

42   Use with pages 141–142.

Visual Thinking

Write how many of each food is in the garden.
Find each sum.

$\begin{array}{r} 3 \\ + 5 \\ \hline 8 \end{array}$

$\begin{array}{r} 5 \\ + 5 \\ \hline 10 \end{array}$

$\begin{array}{r} 7 \\ + 5 \\ \hline 12 \end{array}$

$\begin{array}{r} 6 \\ + 5 \\ \hline 11 \end{array}$

$\begin{array}{r} 4 \\ + 5 \\ \hline 9 \end{array}$

Notes for Home Your child found sums with 5 as an addend. *Home Activity:* Ask your child to use his or her fingers to count on (forward) 5 to find the sum of a large number and 5, for example 87 + 5. (92)

Use with pages 143–144. **43**

Critical Thinking

Show the children to their seats.
Use the clues the children give you.
For each child, write his or her name below the correct seat.

Lee: My seat number is less than 12 and more than 10.

Laura: My seat number is more than 6 and less than 10.
It is even.

Kim: My seat number is more than 8 and less than 11.
It is odd.

Stacy: My seat number is more than 9 and less than 12.
It is even.

Robert: My seat number is less than 9 and more than 6.
It is odd.

7   8   9   10   11   12

Robert   Laura   Kim   Stacy   Lee

Notes for Home Your child used logical thinking to discover unknown numbers. *Home Activity:* Ask your child to guess a number you have chosen. Give him or her clues like the ones on this page which will lead to one correct answer.

44   Use with pages 145–146.

155

Decision Making

Extend Your Thinking 4-8

Everyone must be off when the elevator gets to the bottom!

Only 0, 1, or 2 people get off at each floor.

At each stop, fill in the boxes and circles.

Answers in column 2 will vary.

Floors | People

$10 - 1 = 9$ $12 - 0 = 12$

$9 - 1 = 8$ $12 - \underline{} = \bigcirc$

$8 - 1 = 7$ $\bigcirc - \underline{} = \bigcirc$

$7 - 1 = 6$ $\bigcirc - \underline{} = \bigcirc$

$6 - 1 = 5$ $\bigcirc - \underline{} = \bigcirc$

$5 - 1 = 4$ $\bigcirc - \underline{} = \bigcirc$

$4 - 1 = 3$ $\bigcirc - \underline{} = \bigcirc$

$3 - 1 = 2$ $\bigcirc - \underline{} = \bigcirc$

$2 - 1 = 1$ $\bigcirc - \underline{} = \bigcirc$

$1 - 1 = 0$ $\bigcirc - \underline{} = \bigcirc$

Notes for Home Your child subtracted 0, 1, or 2 from 12 and numbers below 12. *Home Activity:* Ask your child to read the subtraction sentences aloud in the People column.

Use with pages 149–150. **45**

Visual Thinking

Extend Your Thinking 4-9

What did Mama Bear say to Billy Bear?

Here's how to find out.

Solve each problem. Write the answer.

Match the answer to a letter from the list.

Write the letter on the line.

A = 1	F = 4	N = 7	U = 10
D = 2	H = 5	O = 8	V = 11
E = 3	K = 6	R = 9	W = 12

W $12 - 0 = 12$ O $9 - 1 = 8$ R $11 - 2 = 9$ K $7 - 1 = 6$

H $7 - 2 = 5$ A $1 - 0 = 1$ R $10 - 1 = 9$ D $4 - 2 = 2$

H $6 - 1 = 5$ A $3 - 2 = 1$ V $12 - 1 = 11$ E $5 - 2 = 3$

F $6 - 2 = 4$ U $11 - 1 = 10$ N $9 - 2 = 7$

Notes for Home Your child counted back by 0, 1, or 2 to solve subtraction facts and matched answers to letters to crack a code. *Home Activity:* For one of the given number sentences, ask your child to think of another number sentence that would have the same answer. For example, for 9 − 2 = 7, an alternate might be 8 − 1 = 7.

46 Use with pages 151–152.

Visual Thinking

Extend Your Thinking 4-10

Find the differences.

If you subtract 0, color that part of the pattern blue.

If the answer is 0, color that part of the pattern red.

If 0 is NOT in the problem at all, do not color that part.

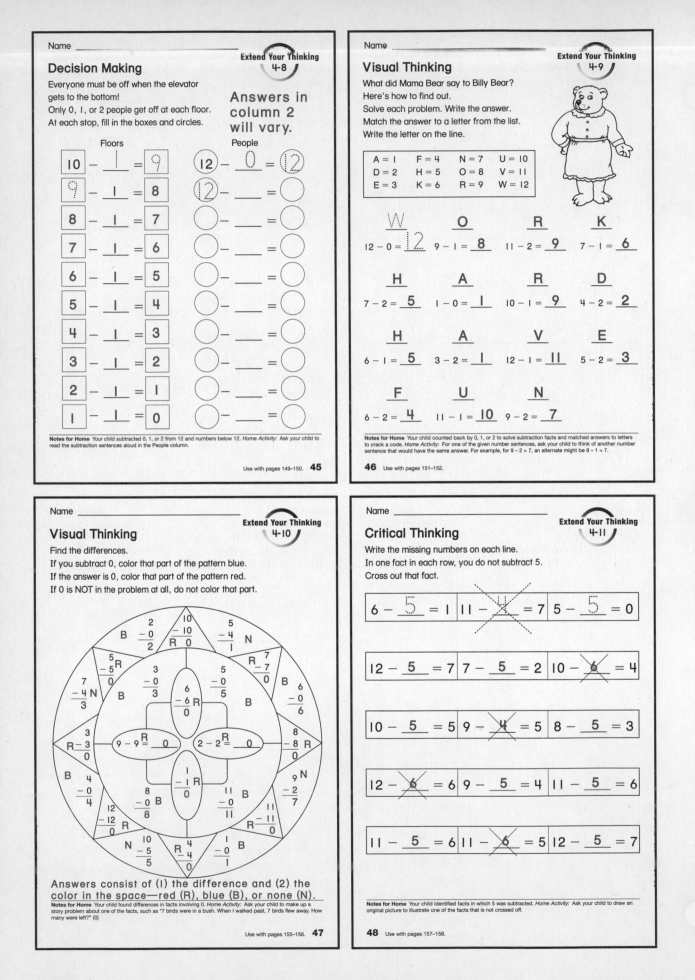

Answers consist of (1) the difference and (2) the color in the space—red (R), blue (B), or none (N).

Notes for Home Your child found differences in facts involving 0. *Home Activity:* Ask your child to make up a story problem about one of the facts, such as "7 birds were in a bush. When I walked past, 7 birds flew away. How many were left?" (0)

Use with pages 155–156. **47**

Critical Thinking

Extend Your Thinking 4-11

Write the missing numbers on each line.

In one fact in each row, you do not subtract 5.

Cross out that fact.

$6 - 5 = 1$	$11 - 4 = 7$ (crossed out)	$5 - 5 = 0$
$12 - 5 = 7$	$7 - 5 = 2$	$10 - 6 = 4$ (crossed out)
$10 - 5 = 5$	$9 - 4 = 5$ (crossed out)	$8 - 5 = 3$
$12 - 6 = 6$ (crossed out)	$9 - 5 = 4$	$11 - 5 = 6$
$11 - 5 = 6$	$11 - 6 = 5$ (crossed out)	$12 - 5 = 7$

Notes for Home Your child identified facts in which 5 was subtracted. *Home Activity:* Ask your child to draw an original picture to illustrate one of the facts that is not crossed off.

48 Use with pages 157–158.

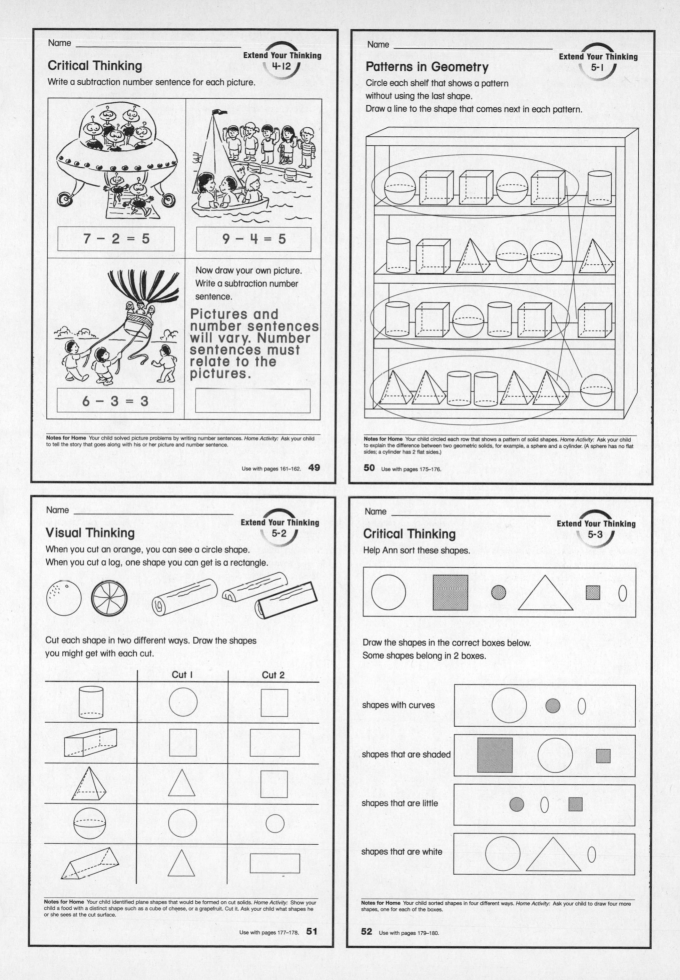

Critical Thinking

Write a subtraction number sentence for each picture.

7 − 2 = 5

9 − 4 = 5

Now draw your own picture.
Write a subtraction number sentence.

Pictures and number sentences will vary. Number sentences must relate to the pictures.

6 − 3 = 3

Notes for Home Your child solved picture problems by writing number sentences. *Home Activity:* Ask your child to tell the story that goes along with his or her picture and number sentence.

Use with pages 161–162. **49**

Patterns in Geometry

Circle each shelf that shows a pattern without using the last shape.
Draw a line to the shape that comes next in each pattern.

Notes for Home Your child circled each row that shows a pattern of solid shapes. *Home Activity:* Ask your child to explain the difference between two geometric solids, for example, a sphere and a cylinder. (A sphere has no flat sides; a cylinder has 2 flat sides.)

50 Use with pages 175–176.

Visual Thinking

When you cut an orange, you can see a circle shape.
When you cut a log, one shape you can get is a rectangle.

Cut each shape in two different ways. Draw the shapes you might get with each cut.

	Cut 1	Cut 2
	○	□
	□	□
	△	□
	○	○
	△	▭

Notes for Home Your child identified plane shapes that would be formed on cut solids. *Home Activity:* Show your child a food with a distinct shape such as a cube of cheese, or a grapefruit. Cut it. Ask your child what shapes he or she sees at the cut surface.

Use with pages 177–178. **51**

Critical Thinking

Help Ann sort these shapes.

Draw the shapes in the correct boxes below.
Some shapes belong in 2 boxes.

shapes with curves

shapes that are shaded

shapes that are little

shapes that are white

Notes for Home Your child sorted shapes in four different ways. *Home Activity:* Ask your child to draw four more shapes, one for each of the boxes.

52 Use with pages 179–180.

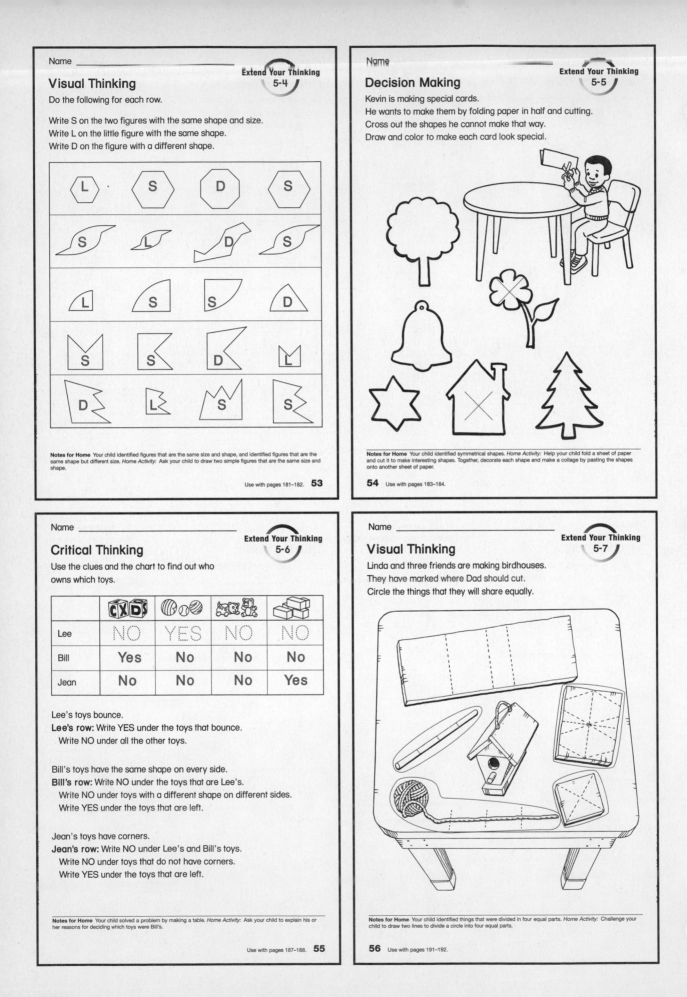

Visual Thinking

Do the following for each row.

Write S on the two figures with the same shape and size.

Write L on the little figure with the same shape.

Write D on the figure with a different shape.

L	S	D	S
S	L	D	S
L	S	S	D
S	S	D	L
D	L	S	S

Notes for Home Your child identified figures that are the same size and shape, and identified figures that are the same shape but different size. *Home Activity:* Ask your child to draw two simple figures that are the same size and shape.

Use with pages 181–182. **53**

Decision Making

Kevin is making special cards.

He wants to make them by folding paper in half and cutting.

Cross out the shapes he cannot make that way.

Draw and color to make each card look special.

Notes for Home Your child identified symmetrical shapes. *Home Activity:* Help your child fold a sheet of paper and cut it to make interesting shapes. Together, decorate each shape and make a collage by pasting the shapes onto another sheet of paper.

54 Use with pages 183–184.

Critical Thinking

Use the clues and the chart to find out who owns which toys.

	CXDS	⚬⚬⚬	🐱🐻	▦
Lee	NO	YES	NO	NO
Bill	Yes	No	No	No
Jean	No	No	No	Yes

Lee's toys bounce.

Lee's row: Write YES under the toys that bounce.
   Write NO under all the other toys.

Bill's toys have the same shape on every side.

Bill's row: Write NO under the toys that are Lee's.
   Write NO under toys with a different shape on different sides.
   Write YES under the toys that are left.

Jean's toys have corners.

Jean's row: Write NO under Lee's and Bill's toys.
   Write NO under toys that do not have corners.
   Write YES under the toys that are left.

Notes for Home Your child solved a problem by making a table. *Home Activity:* Ask your child to explain his or her reasons for deciding which toys were Bill's.

Use with pages 187–188. **55**

Visual Thinking

Linda and three friends are making birdhouses.

They have marked where Dad should cut.

Circle the things that they will share equally.

Notes for Home Your child identified things that were divided in four equal parts. *Home Activity:* Challenge your child to draw two lines to divide a circle into four equal parts.

56 Use with pages 191–192.

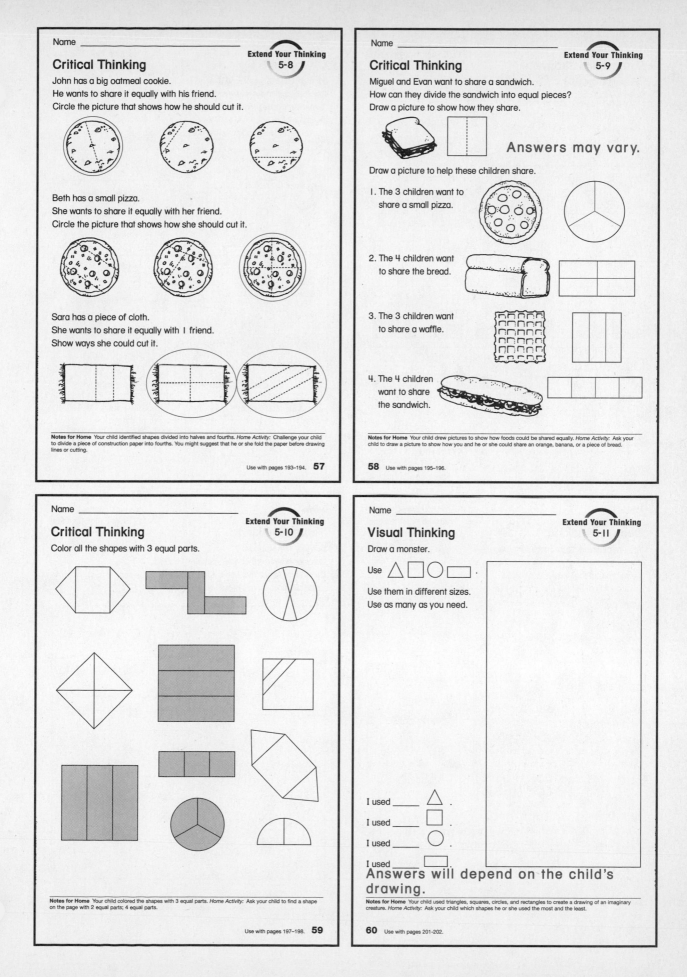

Name _____

Critical Thinking

John has a big oatmeal cookie.
He wants to share it equally with his friend.
Circle the picture that shows how he should cut it.

Beth has a small pizza.
She wants to share it equally with her friend.
Circle the picture that shows how she should cut it.

Sara has a piece of cloth.
She wants to share it equally with 1 friend.
Show ways she could cut it.

Notes for Home Your child identified shapes divided into halves and fourths. *Home Activity:* Challenge your child to divide a piece of construction paper into fourths. You might suggest that he or she fold the paper before drawing lines or cutting.

Use with pages 193–194. **57**

Name _____

Critical Thinking

Miguel and Evan want to share a sandwich.
How can they divide the sandwich into equal pieces?
Draw a picture to show how they share.

Answers may vary.

Draw a picture to help these children share.

1. The 3 children want to share a small pizza.

2. The 4 children want to share the bread.

3. The 3 children want to share a waffle.

4. The 4 children want to share the sandwich.

Notes for Home Your child drew pictures to show how foods could be shared equally. *Home Activity:* Ask your child to draw a picture to show how you and he or she could share an orange, banana, or a piece of bread.

58 Use with pages 195–196.

Name _____

Critical Thinking

Color all the shapes with 3 equal parts.

Notes for Home Your child colored the shapes with 3 equal parts. *Home Activity:* Ask your child to find a shape on the page with 2 equal parts; 4 equal parts.

Use with pages 197–198. **59**

Name _____

Visual Thinking

Draw a monster.

Use △ ☐ ◯ ▭ .

Use them in different sizes.
Use as many as you need.

I used _____ △ .

I used _____ ☐ .

I used _____ ◯ .

I used _____ ▭ .

Answers will depend on the child's drawing.

Notes for Home Your child used triangles, squares, circles, and rectangles to create a drawing of an imaginary creature. *Home Activity:* Ask your child which shapes he or she used the most and the least.

60 Use with pages 201–202.

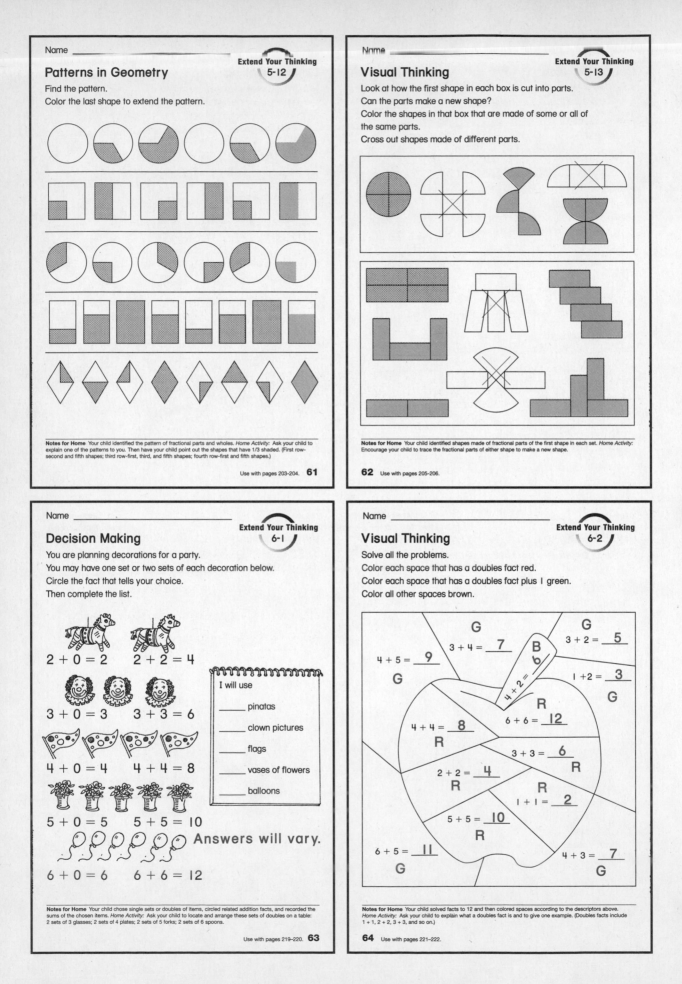

Patterns in Geometry

Find the pattern.
Color the last shape to extend the pattern.

Notes for Home Your child identified the pattern of fractional parts and wholes. *Home Activity:* Ask your child to explain one of the patterns to you. Then have your child point out the shapes that have 1/3 shaded. (First row-second and fifth shapes; third row-first, third, and fifth shapes; fourth row-first and fifth shapes.)

Use with pages 203-204. **61**

Visual Thinking

Look at how the first shape in each box is cut into parts.
Can the parts make a new shape?
Color the shapes in that box that are made of some or all of the same parts.
Cross out shapes made of different parts.

Notes for Home Your child identified shapes made of fractional parts of the first shape in each set. *Home Activity:* Encourage your child to trace the fractional parts of either shape to make a new shape.

62 Use with pages 205-206.

Decision Making

You are planning decorations for a party.
You may have one set or two sets of each decoration below.
Circle the fact that tells your choice.
Then complete the list.

2 + 0 = 2   2 + 2 = 4

3 + 0 = 3   3 + 3 = 6

4 + 0 = 4   4 + 4 = 8

5 + 0 = 5   5 + 5 = 10

6 + 0 = 6   6 + 6 = 12

I will use

_____ pinatas

_____ clown pictures

_____ flags

_____ vases of flowers

_____ balloons

Answers will vary.

Notes for Home Your child chose single sets or doubles of items, circled related addition facts, and recorded the sums of the chosen items. *Home Activity:* Ask your child to locate and arrange these sets of doubles on a table: 2 sets of 3 glasses; 2 sets of 4 plates; 2 sets of 5 forks; 2 sets of 6 spoons.

Use with pages 219-220. **63**

Visual Thinking

Solve all the problems.
Color each space that has a doubles fact red.
Color each space that has a doubles fact plus 1 green.
Color all other spaces brown.

G   3 + 4 = 7   B   G   3 + 2 = 5

4 + 5 = 9   b   1 + 2 = 3

G   4 + 2 =   R   G

4 + 4 = 8   6 + 6 = 12

R   3 + 3 = 6

2 + 2 = 4   R

R   R   1 + 1 = 2

5 + 5 = 10

R

6 + 5 = 11   4 + 3 = 7

G   G

Notes for Home Your child solved facts to 12 and then colored spaces according to the descriptors above. *Home Activity:* Ask your child to explain what a doubles fact is and to give one example. (Doubles facts include 1 + 1, 2 + 2, 3 + 3, and so on.)

64 Use with pages 221-222.

Name _____

Critical Thinking

Solve each problem.
Circle the answers that show a doubles fact.
Box the answers that show a doubles fact plus 1.

1. Myra bought 6 erasers. Kathy bought the same amount.

   How many erasers do they have together? $\boxed{6 + 6 = 12}$ (circled)

2. Robert found 5 pennies. John found 6 pennies.

   How many pennies did they find in all? $\boxed{5 + 6 = 11}$

3. Alice brought home 2 kittens. Grace brought home 4 more.

   How many kittens do they have at home now? $2 + 4 = 6$

4. Mark jumped across 4 puddles. Laura jumped across
   3 other puddles. How many puddles did they jump in all?

   $\boxed{4 + 3 = 7}$

5. Farmer Bob had some carrots. He fed Rigby Rabbit 2 carrots. He
   also fed Molly Mule 2 carrots. Now he has no carrots.

   How many carrots did Farmer Bob have? (circled) $2 + 2 = 4$

Notes for Home Your child solved addition problems and identified doubles facts and doubles facts plus 1.
Home Activity: Ask your child to create another problem that illustrates a doubles fact plus 1.
(For example: 3 + 4 = 7.)

Name _____

Decision Making

Solve the addition facts. Read the problem.
Circle the addition doubles fact that helps solve each problem.
Then write the subtraction fact that answers each problem.

1. $3 + 3 =$ __6__ $4 + 4 =$ __8__   (circled) $5 + 5 =$ __10__

   Frank stood on his head for 5 seconds.

   Rick stood on his head for 10 seconds.

   How much longer did Rick stand on his head?

   $\underline{10 - 5 = 5;\ 5\ \text{seconds}}$

2. $6 + 6 =$ __12__   (circled) $4 + 4 =$ __8__ $8 + 8 =$ __16__

   Myra did 8 jumping jacks. Nan did 4.

   How many more did Myra do? $\underline{8 - 4 = 4;\ 4\ \text{more}}$

Create your own problem to match 1 of the addition doubles facts
shown below. Write a subtraction fact to go with the story.

Answers will vary.

$5 + 5 =$ _____ $6 + 6 =$ _____ $3 + 3 =$ _____

On Tuesday, I _____. I did this _____ times.

On Wednesday, I did it _____ times.

How many more times did I do it on _____ than on

_____ ? _____ − _____ = _____

Notes for Home Your child used addition doubles facts to help solve word problems involving subtraction.
Home Activity: Ask your child to create another problem for you to solve.

Name _____

Critical Thinking

Mr. Johnson's class voted on the place the children most
wanted to visit.

1. Which place do the most children want to visit? **Ocean**

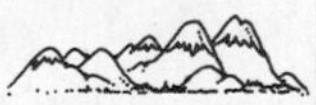

2. How many children in this class live near the (ocean)?

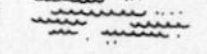

   You can't tell from this chart.

3. How many more children voted to visit the (desert)

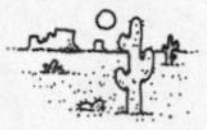

   than the (mountains)? __3__

4. Which place gets the least visitors every year?

   You can't tell from this chart.

5. How many children would like to visit the (mountains)? __5__

Notes for Home Your child decided whether a given set of data would help answer related questions.
Home Activity: Ask your child to explain why the questions can or cannot be answered using only the data given
on the chart.

Name _____

Visual Thinking

You need a coin and a marker.
Put your marker on START. Toss the coin.

Heads: Go to the next fact with all 3 numbers the same
as on the space with your marker.

Tails: Go to the next fact with at least 1 different number.

Move your marker. Repeat until you get to the END.
How many turns did you need to get to END? _____ turns.

Answers will vary.

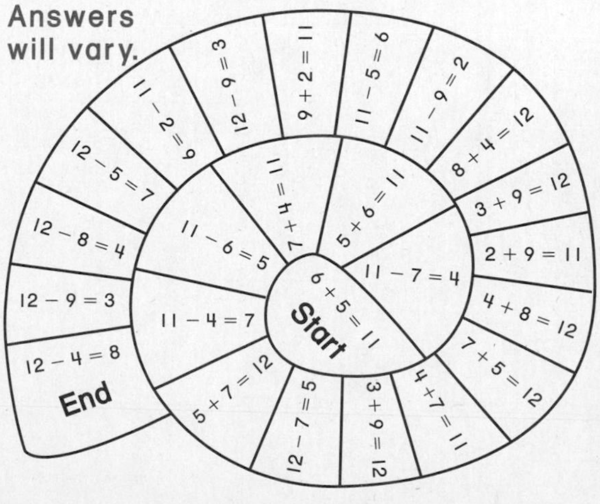

Notes for Home Your child identified related facts by moving his or her marker along a game board.
Home Activity: Ask your child to state related subtraction facts for these addition facts: 3 + 3 = 6 (6 − 3 = 3),
4 + 4 = 8 (8 − 4 = 4), and 5 + 5 = 10 (10 − 5 = 5).

Critical Thinking

Extend Your Thinking 6-7

The fact families are having a picnic.

Color the ones that belong to this family [brown] : 6 + 5 = 11.

Color the ones that belong to this family [orange] : 4 + 8 = 12.

Color the ones that belong to this family [gray] : 10 − 3 = 7.

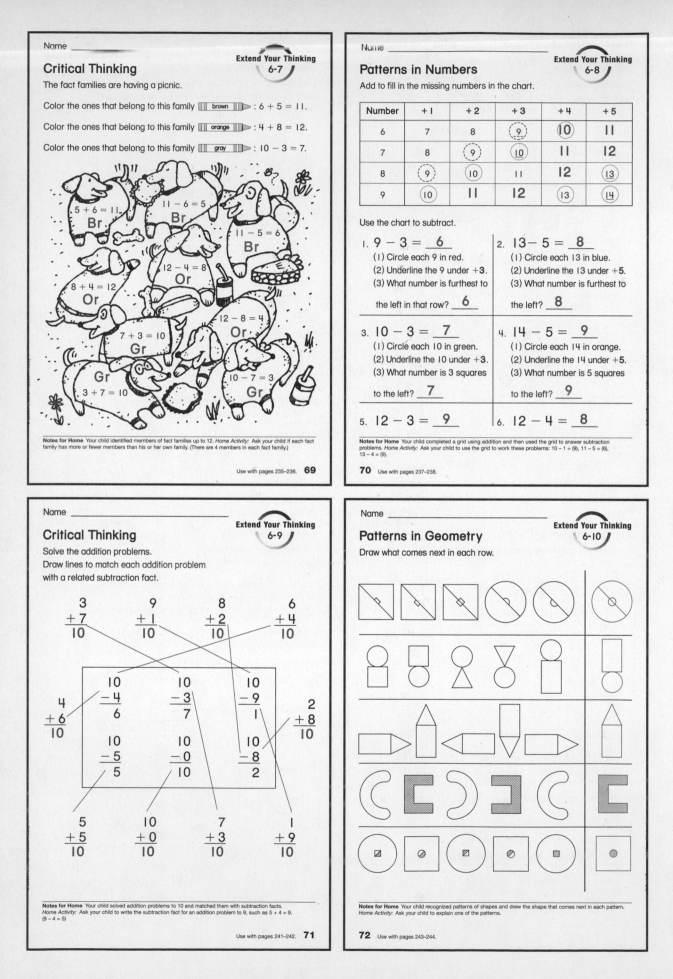

5 + 6 = 11 Br

11 − 6 = 5 Br

11 − 5 = 6 Br

12 − 4 = 8 Or

8 + 4 = 12 Or

12 − 8 = 4 Or

7 + 3 = 10 Gr

Gr

3 + 7 = 10 Gr

10 − 7 = 3 Gr

Notes for Home Your child identified members of fact families up to 12. *Home Activity:* Ask your child if each fact family has more or fewer members than his or her own family. (There are 4 members in each fact family.)

Use with pages 235–236. **69**

Patterns in Numbers

Extend Your Thinking 6-8

Add to fill in the missing numbers in the chart.

Number	+ 1	+ 2	+ 3	+ 4	+ 5
6	7	8	(9)	(10)	11
7	8	(9)	(10)	11	12
8	(9)	(10)	11	12	(13)
9	(10)	11	12	(13)	(14)

Use the chart to subtract.

1. 9 − 3 = __6__
   (1) Circle each 9 in red.
   (2) Underline the 9 under +3.
   (3) What number is furthest to the left in that row? __6__

2. 13 − 5 = __8__
   (1) Circle each 13 in blue.
   (2) Underline the 13 under +5.
   (3) What number is furthest to the left? __8__

3. 10 − 3 = __7__
   (1) Circle each 10 in green.
   (2) Underline the 10 under +3.
   (3) What number is 3 squares to the left? __7__

4. 14 − 5 = __9__
   (1) Circle each 14 in orange.
   (2) Underline the 14 under +5.
   (3) What number is 5 squares to the left? __9__

5. 12 − 3 = __9__

6. 12 − 4 = __8__

Notes for Home Your child completed a grid using addition and then used the grid to answer subtraction problems. *Home Activity:* Ask your child to use the grid to work these problems: 10 − 1 = (9), 11 − 5 = (6), 13 − 4 = (9).

70 Use with pages 237–238.

Critical Thinking

Extend Your Thinking 6-9

Solve the addition problems.
Draw lines to match each addition problem with a related subtraction fact.

3 + 7 = 10

9 + 1 = 10

8 + 2 = 10

6 + 4 = 10

4 + 6 = 10

2 + 8 = 10

10 − 4 = 6

10 − 3 = 7

10 − 9 = 1

10 − 5 = 5

10 − 0 = 10

10 − 8 = 2

5 + 5 = 10

10 + 0 = 10

7 + 3 = 10

1 + 9 = 10

Notes for Home Your child solved addition problems to 10 and matched them with subtraction facts. *Home Activity:* Ask your child to write the subtraction fact for an addition problem to 9, such as 5 + 4 = 9. (9 − 4 = 5)

Use with pages 241–242. **71**

Patterns in Geometry

Extend Your Thinking 6-10

Draw what comes next in each row.

Notes for Home Your child recognized patterns of shapes and drew the shape that comes next in each pattern. *Home Activity:* Ask your child to explain one of the patterns.

72 Use with pages 243–244.

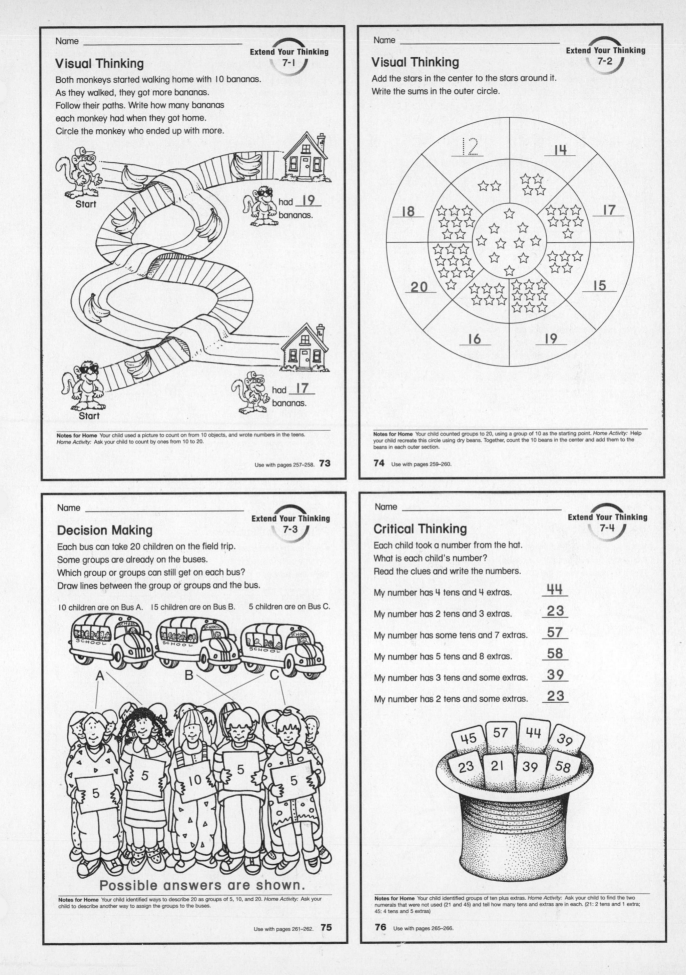

Name _____

Visual Thinking

Both monkeys started walking home with 10 bananas.
As they walked, they got more bananas.
Follow their paths. Write how many bananas
each monkey had when they got home.
Circle the monkey who ended up with more.

Start

had 19 bananas.

Start

had 17 bananas.

Notes for Home Your child used a picture to count on from 10 objects, and wrote numbers in the teens. *Home Activity:* Ask your child to count by ones from 10 to 20.

Use with pages 257–258. **73**

Name _____

Visual Thinking

Add the stars in the center to the stars around it.
Write the sums in the outer circle.

12   14

18   17

20   15

16   19

Notes for Home Your child counted groups to 20, using a group of 10 as the starting point. *Home Activity:* Help your child recreate this circle using dry beans. Together, count the 10 beans in the center and add them to the beans in each outer section.

74 Use with pages 259–260.

Name _____

Decision Making

Each bus can take 20 children on the field trip.
Some groups are already on the buses.
Which group or groups can still get on each bus?
Draw lines between the group or groups and the bus.

10 children are on Bus A.   15 children are on Bus B.   5 children are on Bus C.

A   B   C

5   5   10   5   5

Possible answers are shown.

Notes for Home Your child identified ways to describe 20 as groups of 5, 10, and 20. *Home Activity:* Ask your child to describe another way to assign the groups to the buses.

Use with pages 261–262. **75**

Name _____

Critical Thinking

Each child took a number from the hat.
What is each child's number?
Read the clues and write the numbers.

My number has 4 tens and 4 extras. ___44___

My number has 2 tens and 3 extras. ___23___

My number has some tens and 7 extras. ___57___

My number has 5 tens and 8 extras. ___58___

My number has 3 tens and some extras. ___39___

My number has 2 tens and some extras. ___23___

45   57   44   39

23   21   39   58

Notes for Home Your child identified groups of ten plus extras. *Home Activity:* Ask your child to find the two numerals that were not used (21 and 45) and tell how many tens and extras are in each. (21: 2 tens and 1 extra; 45: 4 tens and 5 extras)

76 Use with pages 265–266.

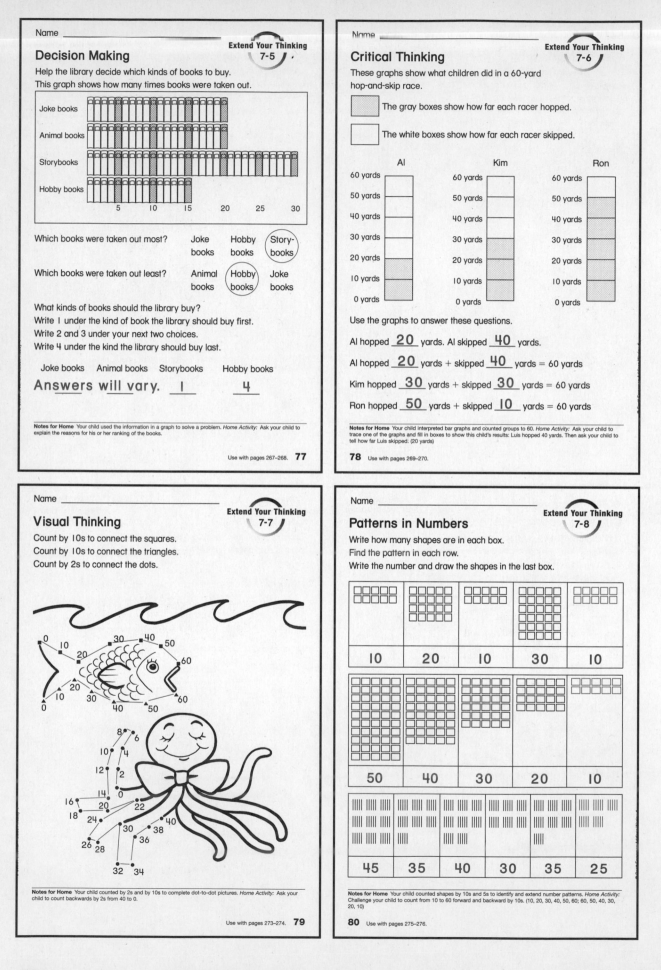

Decision Making

Help the library decide which kinds of books to buy.
This graph shows how many times books were taken out.

Joke books
Animal books
Storybooks
Hobby books

5   10   15   20   25   30

Which books were taken out most?   Joke books   Hobby books   (Story-books)

Which books were taken out least?   Animal books   (Hobby books)   Joke books

What kinds of books should the library buy?
Write 1 under the kind of book the library should buy first.
Write 2 and 3 under your next two choices.
Write 4 under the kind the library should buy last.

Joke books   Animal books   Storybooks   Hobby books

Answers will vary.   1   4

Notes for Home Your child used the information in a graph to solve a problem. Home Activity: Ask your child to explain the reasons for his or her ranking of the books.

Use with pages 267–268.   **77**

Critical Thinking

These graphs show what children did in a 60-yard hop-and-skip race.

The gray boxes show how far each racer hopped.

The white boxes show how far each racer skipped.

Al   Kim   Ron

60 yards   60 yards   60 yards
50 yards   50 yards   50 yards
40 yards   40 yards   40 yards
30 yards   30 yards   30 yards
20 yards   20 yards   20 yards
10 yards   10 yards   10 yards
0 yards   0 yards   0 yards

Use the graphs to answer these questions.

Al hopped __20__ yards. Al skipped __40__ yards.

Al hopped __20__ yards + skipped __40__ yards = 60 yards

Kim hopped __30__ yards + skipped __30__ yards = 60 yards

Ron hopped __50__ yards + skipped __10__ yards = 60 yards

Notes for Home Your child interpreted bar graphs and counted groups to 60. Home Activity: Ask your child to trace one of the graphs and fill in boxes to show this child's results: Luis hopped 40 yards. Then ask your child to tell how far Luis skipped. (20 yards)

78   Use with pages 269–270.

Visual Thinking

Count by 10s to connect the squares.
Count by 10s to connect the triangles.
Count by 2s to connect the dots.

Notes for Home Your child counted by 2s and by 10s to complete dot-to-dot pictures. Home Activity: Ask your child to count backwards by 2s from 40 to 0.

Use with pages 273–274.   **79**

Patterns in Numbers

Write how many shapes are in each box.
Find the pattern in each row.
Write the number and draw the shapes in the last box.

10   20   10   30   10

50   40   30   20   10

45   35   40   30   35   25

Notes for Home Your child counted shapes by 10s and 5s to identify and extend number patterns. Home Activity: Challenge your child to count from 10 to 60 forward and backward by 10s. (10, 20, 30, 40, 50, 60; 60, 50, 40, 30, 20, 10)

80   Use with pages 275–276.

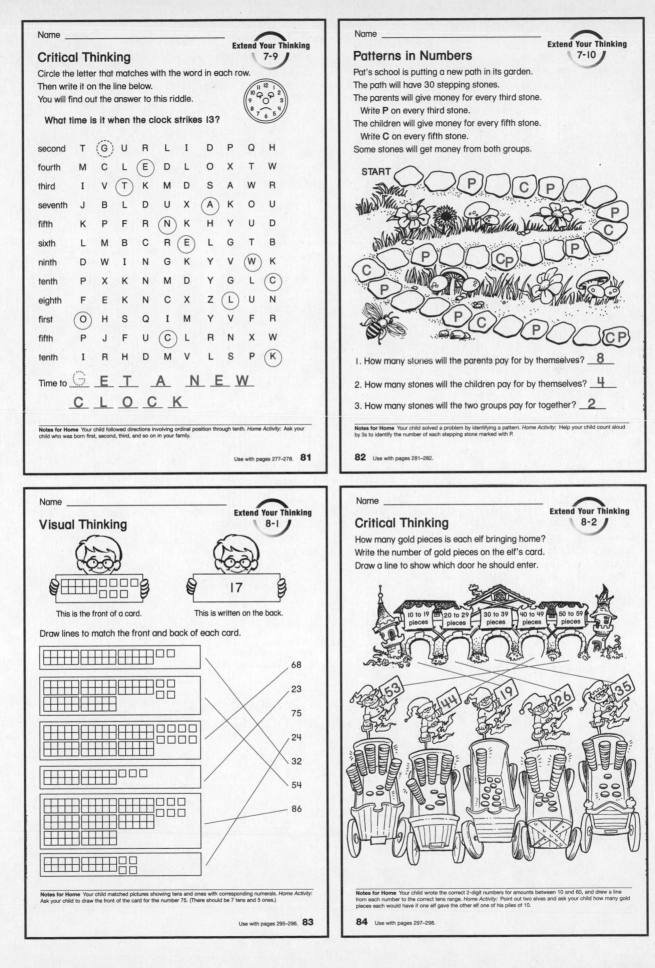

Panel 1 (top-left)

Name _____

Critical Thinking

Circle the letter that matches with the word in each row.
Then write it on the line below.
You will find out the answer to this riddle.

What time is it when the clock strikes 13?

second	T	(G)	U	R	L	I	D	P	Q	H
fourth	M	C	L	(E)	D	L	O	X	T	W
third	I	V	(T)	K	M	D	S	A	W	R
seventh	J	B	L	D	U	X	(A)	K	O	U
fifth	K	P	F	R	(N)	K	H	Y	U	D
sixth	L	M	B	C	R	(E)	L	G	T	B
ninth	D	W	I	N	G	K	Y	V	(W)	K
tenth	P	X	K	N	M	D	Y	G	L	(C)
eighth	F	E	K	N	C	X	Z	(L)	U	N
first	(O)	H	S	Q	I	M	Y	V	F	R
fifth	P	J	F	U	(C)	L	R	N	X	W
tenth	I	R	H	D	M	V	L	S	P	(K)

Time to G E T   A   N E W
C L O C K

Notes for Home Your child followed directions involving ordinal position through tenth. *Home Activity:* Ask your child who was born first, second, third, and so on in your family.

Use with pages 277–278. **81**

Panel 2 (top-right)

Name _____

Patterns in Numbers

Pat's school is putting a new path in its garden.
The path will have 30 stepping stones.
The parents will give money for every third stone.
   Write **P** on every third stone.
The children will give money for every fifth stone.
   Write **C** on every fifth stone.
Some stones will get money from both groups.

START

1. How many stones will the parents pay for by themselves? __8__

2. How many stones will the children pay for by themselves? __4__

3. How many stones will the two groups pay for together? __2__

Notes for Home Your child solved a problem by identifying a pattern. *Home Activity:* Help your child count aloud by 3s to identify the number of each stepping stone marked with P.

82 Use with pages 281–282.

Panel 3 (bottom-left)

Name _____

Visual Thinking

This is the front of a card.   17   This is written on the back.

Draw lines to match the front and back of each card.

68
23
75
24
32
54
86

Notes for Home Your child matched pictures showing tens and ones with corresponding numerals. *Home Activity:* Ask your child to draw the front of the card for the number 75. (There should be 7 tens and 5 ones.)

Use with pages 295–296. **83**

Panel 4 (bottom-right)

Name _____

Critical Thinking

How many gold pieces is each elf bringing home?
Write the number of gold pieces on the elf's card.
Draw a line to show which door he should enter.

10 to 19 pieces   20 to 29 pieces   30 to 39 pieces   40 to 49 pieces   50 to 59 pieces

53   44   19   26   35

Notes for Home Your child wrote the correct 2-digit numbers for amounts between 10 and 60, and drew a line from each number to the correct tens range. *Home Activity:* Point out two elves and ask your child how many gold pieces each would have if one elf gave the other elf one of his piles of 10.

84 Use with pages 297–298.

165

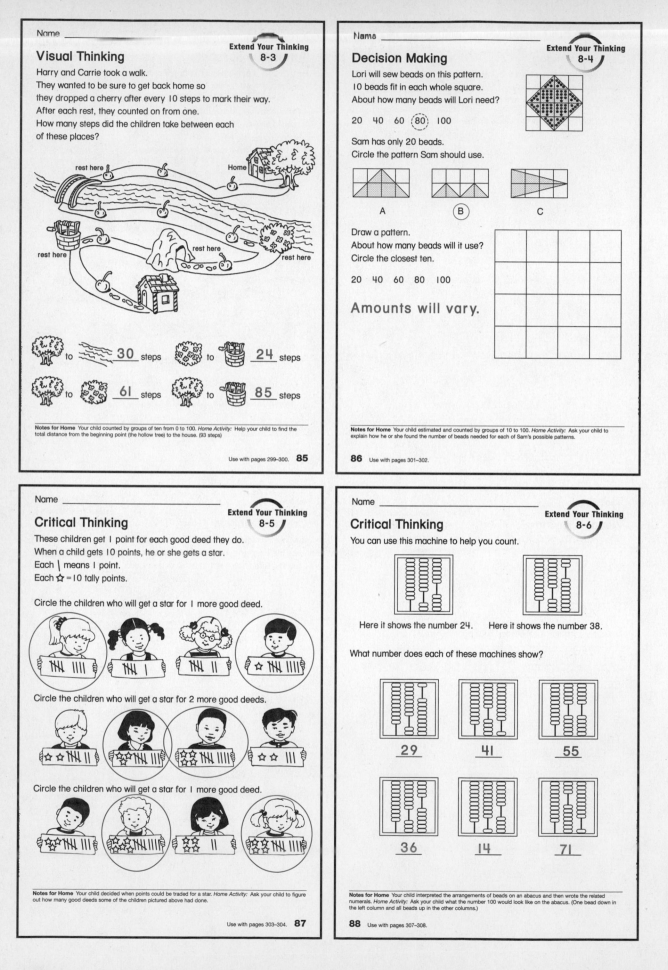

Visual Thinking

Harry and Carrie took a walk.
They wanted to be sure to get back home so
they dropped a cherry after every 10 steps to mark their way.
After each rest, they counted on from one.
How many steps did the children take between each
of these places?

rest here

Home

rest here

rest here

rest here

🌳 to 〰️〰️ __30__ steps   🌸 to 🪣 __24__ steps

🌳 to 🌼 __61__ steps   🌳 to 🪣 __85__ steps

Notes for Home Your child counted by groups of ten from 0 to 100. Home Activity: Help your child to find the
total distance from the beginning point (the hollow tree) to the house. (93 steps)

Use with pages 299–300. **85**

Decision Making

Lori will sew beads on this pattern.
10 beads fit in each whole square.
About how many beads will Lori need?

20   40   60   (80)   100

Sam has only 20 beads.
Circle the pattern Sam should use.

A   (B)   C

Draw a pattern.
About how many beads will it use?
Circle the closest ten.

20   40   60   80   100

Amounts will vary.

Notes for Home Your child estimated and counted by groups of 10 to 100. Home Activity: Ask your child to
explain how he or she found the number of beads needed for each of Sam's possible patterns.

86   Use with pages 301–302.

Critical Thinking

These children get 1 point for each good deed they do.
When a child gets 10 points, he or she gets a star.
Each \ means 1 point.
Each ☆ =10 tally points.

Circle the children who will get a star for 1 more good deed.

Circle the children who will get a star for 2 more good deeds.

Circle the children who will get a star for 1 more good deed.

Notes for Home Your child decided when points could be traded for a star. Home Activity: Ask your child to figure
out how many good deeds some of the children pictured above had done.

Use with pages 303–304. **87**

Critical Thinking

You can use this machine to help you count.

Here it shows the number 24.   Here it shows the number 38.

What number does each of these machines show?

__29__   __41__   __55__

__36__   __14__   __71__

Notes for Home Your child interpreted the arrangements of beads on an abacus and then wrote the related
numerals. Home Activity: Ask your child what the number 100 would look like on the abacus. (One bead down in
the left column and all beads up in the other columns.)

88   Use with pages 307–308.

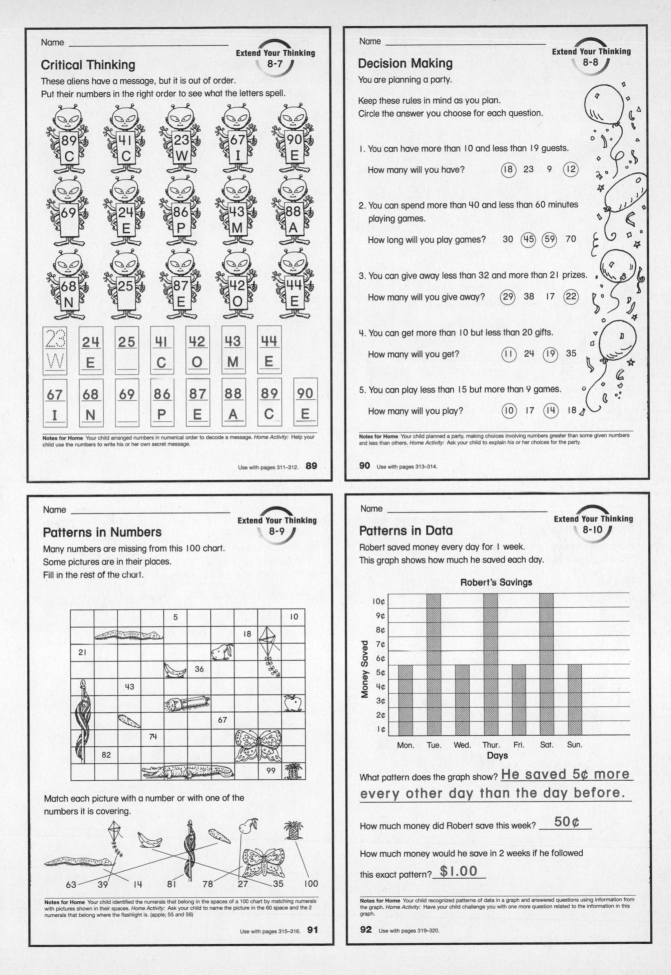

Name _____

Critical Thinking

These aliens have a message, but it is out of order.
Put their numbers in the right order to see what the letters spell.

89 C	41 C	23 W	67 I	90 E
69	24 E	86 P	43 M	88 A
68 N	25	87 E	42 O	44 E

| 23 W | 24 E | 25 | 41 C | 42 O | 43 M | 44 E |
| 67 I | 68 N | 69 | 86 P | 87 E | 88 A | 89 C | 90 E |

Notes for Home Your child arranged numbers in numerical order to decode a message. *Home Activity:* Help your child use the numbers to write his or her own secret message.

Name _____

Decision Making

You are planning a party.

Keep these rules in mind as you plan.
Circle the answer you choose for each question.

1. You can have more than 10 and less than 19 guests.

   How many will you have? (18) 23 9 (12)

2. You can spend more than 40 and less than 60 minutes playing games.

   How long will you play games? 30 (45) (59) 70

3. You can give away less than 32 and more than 21 prizes.

   How many will you give away? (29) 38 17 (22)

4. You can get more than 10 but less than 20 gifts.

   How many will you get? (11) 24 (19) 35

5. You can play less than 15 but more than 9 games.

   How many will you play? (10) 17 (14) 18

Notes for Home Your child planned a party, making choices involving numbers greater than some given numbers and less than others. *Home Activity:* Ask your child to explain his or her choices for the party.

Name _____

Patterns in Numbers

Many numbers are missing from this 100 chart.
Some pictures are in their places.
Fill in the rest of the chart.

Match each picture with a number or with one of the numbers it is covering.

63   39   14   81   78   27   35   100

Notes for Home Your child identified the numerals that belong in the spaces of a 100 chart by matching numerals with pictures shown in their spaces. *Home Activity:* Ask your child to name the picture in the 60 space and the 2 numerals that belong where the flashlight is. (apple; 55 and 56)

Name _____

Patterns in Data

Robert saved money every day for 1 week.
This graph shows how much he saved each day.

Robert's Savings

What pattern does the graph show? **He saved 5¢ more every other day than the day before.**

How much money did Robert save this week? **50¢**

How much money would he save in 2 weeks if he followed this exact pattern? **$1.00**

Notes for Home Your child recognized patterns of data in a graph and answered questions using information from the graph. *Home Activity:* Have your child challenge you with one more question related to the information in this graph.

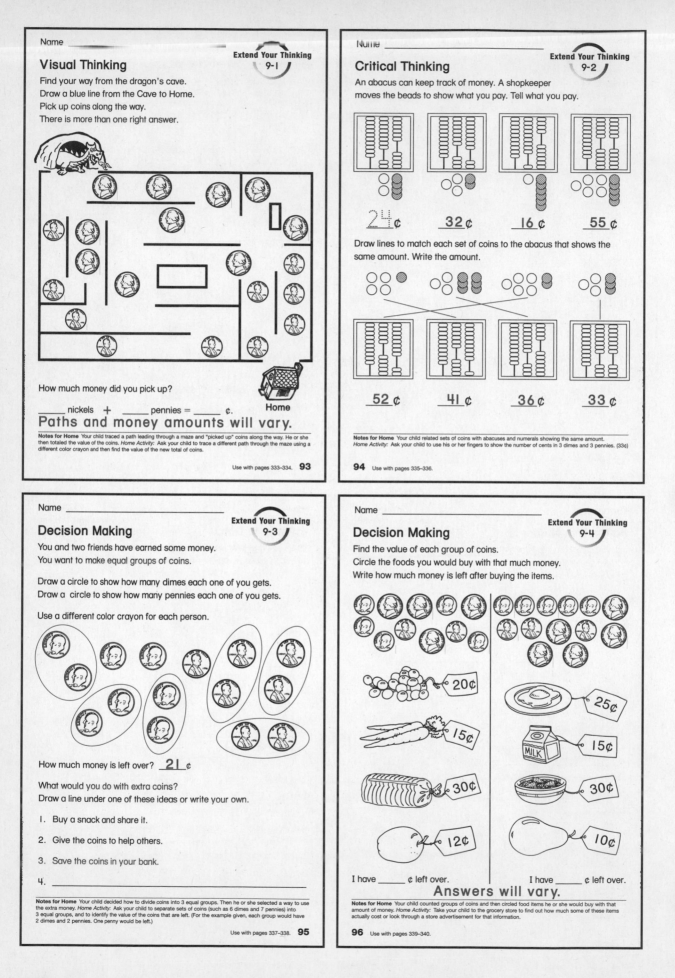

Visual Thinking

Name _____

Find your way from the dragon's cave.
Draw a blue line from the Cave to Home.
Pick up coins along the way.
There is more than one right answer.

How much money did you pick up?

_____ nickels + _____ pennies = _____ ¢.

Paths and money amounts will vary.

Home

Notes for Home Your child traced a path leading through a maze and "picked up" coins along the way. He or she then totaled the value of the coins. *Home Activity:* Ask your child to trace a different path through the maze using a different color crayon and then find the value of the new total of coins.

Use with pages 333–334. **93**

Critical Thinking

Name _____

An abacus can keep track of money. A shopkeeper moves the beads to show what you pay. Tell what you pay.

_24_¢   _32_¢   _16_¢   _55_¢

Draw lines to match each set of coins to the abacus that shows the same amount. Write the amount.

_52_¢   _41_¢   _36_¢   _33_¢

Notes for Home Your child related sets of coins with abacuses and numerals showing the same amount. *Home Activity:* Ask your child to use his or her fingers to show the number of cents in 3 dimes and 3 pennies. (33¢)

94 Use with pages 335–336.

Decision Making

Name _____

You and two friends have earned some money.
You want to make equal groups of coins.

Draw a circle to show how many dimes each one of you gets.
Draw a circle to show how many pennies each one of you gets.

Use a different color crayon for each person.

How much money is left over? _21_ ¢

What would you do with extra coins?
Draw a line under one of these ideas or write your own.

1. Buy a snack and share it.

2. Give the coins to help others.

3. Save the coins in your bank.

4. _____

Notes for Home Your child decided how to divide coins into 3 equal groups. Then he or she selected a way to use the extra money. *Home Activity:* Ask your child to separate sets of coins (such as 6 dimes and 7 pennies) into 3 equal groups, and to identify the value of the coins that are left. (For the example given, each group would have 2 dimes and 2 pennies. One penny would be left.)

Use with pages 337–338. **95**

Decision Making

Name _____

Find the value of each group of coins.
Circle the foods you would buy with that much money.
Write how much money is left after buying the items.

20¢   25¢

15¢   MILK 15¢

30¢   30¢

12¢   10¢

I have _____ ¢ left over.   I have _____ ¢ left over.

Answers will vary.

Notes for Home Your child counted groups of coins and then circled food items he or she would buy with that amount of money. *Home Activity:* Take your child to the grocery store to find out how much some of these items actually cost or look through a store advertisement for that information.

96 Use with pages 339–340.

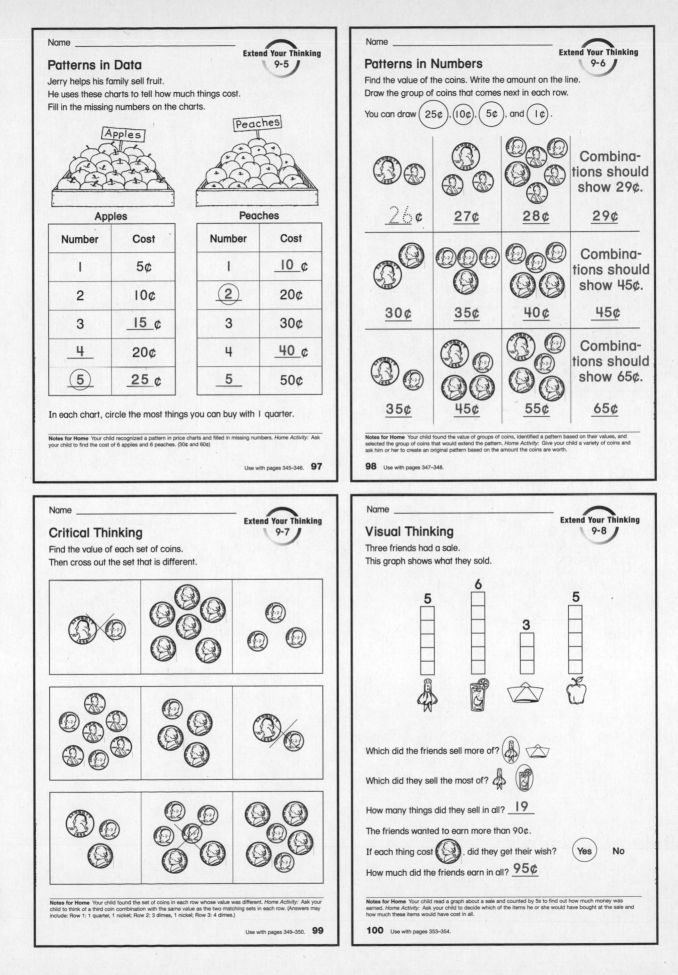

Name _____

Patterns in Data

Jerry helps his family sell fruit.
He uses these charts to tell how much things cost.
Fill in the missing numbers on the charts.

Apples

Peaches

Apples

Number	Cost
1	5¢
2	10¢
3	15¢
4	20¢
5	25¢

Peaches

Number	Cost
1	10¢
2	20¢
3	30¢
4	40¢
5	50¢

In each chart, circle the most things you can buy with 1 quarter.

Notes for Home Your child recognized a pattern in price charts and filled in missing numbers. *Home Activity:* Ask your child to find the cost of 6 apples and 6 peaches. (30¢ and 60¢)

Use with pages 345–346. **97**

Name _____

Patterns in Numbers

Find the value of the coins. Write the amount on the line.
Draw the group of coins that comes next in each row.

You can draw 25¢, 10¢, 5¢, and 1¢.

26¢	27¢	28¢	29¢

Combinations should show 29¢.

30¢	35¢	40¢	45¢

Combinations should show 45¢.

35¢	45¢	55¢	65¢

Combinations should show 65¢.

Notes for Home Your child found the value of groups of coins, identified a pattern based on their values, and selected the group of coins that would extend the pattern. *Home Activity:* Give your child a variety of coins and ask him or her to create an original pattern based on the amount the coins are worth.

98 Use with pages 347–348.

Name _____

Critical Thinking

Find the value of each set of coins.
Then cross out the set that is different.

Notes for Home Your child found the set of coins in each row whose value was different. *Home Activity:* Ask your child to think of a third coin combination with the same value as the two matching sets in each row. (Answers may include: Row 1: 1 quarter, 1 nickel; Row 2: 3 dimes, 1 nickel; Row 3: 4 dimes.)

Use with pages 349–350. **99**

Name _____

Visual Thinking

Three friends had a sale.
This graph shows what they sold.

5	6	3	5

Which did the friends sell more of? ____

Which did they sell the most of? ____

How many things did they sell in all? __19__

The friends wanted to earn more than 90¢.

If each thing cost ⬤, did they get their wish? (Yes) No

How much did the friends earn in all? __95¢__

Notes for Home Your child read a graph about a sale and counted by 5s to find out how much money was earned. *Home Activity:* Ask your child to decide which of the items he or she would have bought at the sale and how much these items would have cost in all.

100 Use with pages 353–354.

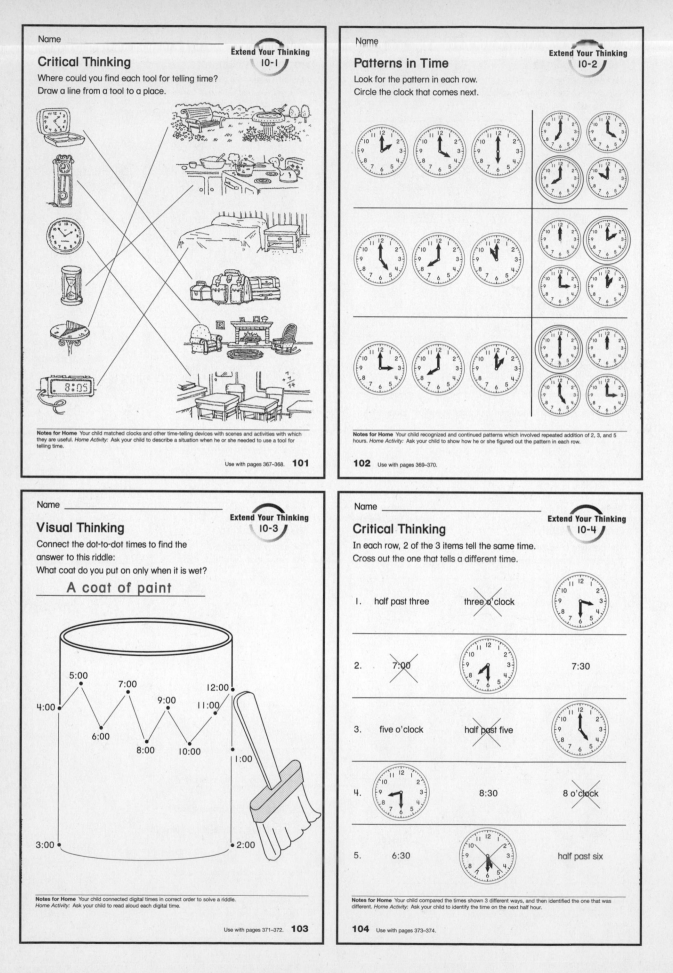

Name _____

Critical Thinking

Extend Your Thinking
10-1

Where could you find each tool for telling time?
Draw a line from a tool to a place.

Use with pages 367–368. **101**

Name _____

Patterns in Time

Extend Your Thinking
10-2

Look for the pattern in each row.
Circle the clock that comes next.

102 Use with pages 369–370.

Name _____

Visual Thinking

Extend Your Thinking
10-3

Connect the dot-to-dot times to find the
answer to this riddle:
What coat do you put on only when it is wet?

A coat of paint

5:00
7:00
12:00
4:00
9:00
11:00
6:00
10:00
8:00
1:00
3:00
2:00

Use with pages 371–372. **103**

Name _____

Critical Thinking

Extend Your Thinking
10-4

In each row, 2 of the 3 items tell the same time.
Cross out the one that tells a different time.

1. half past three   three o'clock

2. 7:00   7:30

3. five o'clock   half past five

4.   8:30   8 o'clock

5. 6:30   half past six

104 Use with pages 373–374.

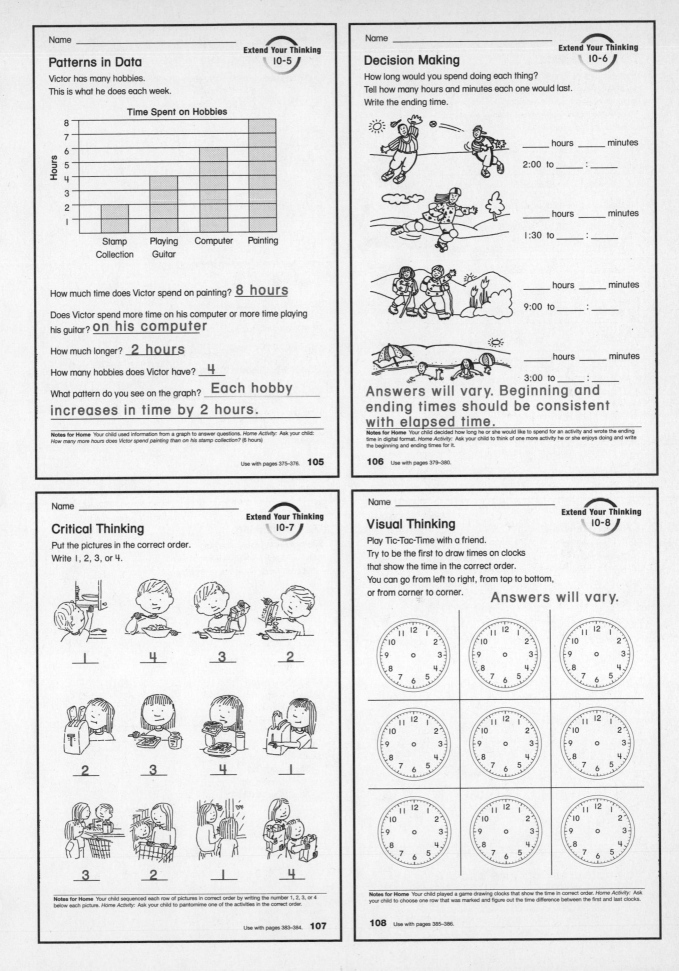

Name _____

Patterns in Data

Victor has many hobbies.
This is what he does each week.

Time Spent on Hobbies

Hours

8
7
6
5
4
3
2
1

Stamp Collection Playing Guitar Computer Painting

How much time does Victor spend on painting? **8 hours**

Does Victor spend more time on his computer or more time playing his guitar? **on his computer**

How much longer? **2 hours**

How many hobbies does Victor have? **4**

What pattern do you see on the graph? **Each hobby increases in time by 2 hours.**

Notes for Home Your child used information from a graph to answer questions. *Home Activity:* Ask your child: *How many more hours does Victor spend painting than on his stamp collection?* (6 hours)

Use with pages 375–376. **105**

Name _____

Decision Making

How long would you spend doing each thing?
Tell how many hours and minutes each one would last.
Write the ending time.

_____ hours _____ minutes
2:00 to _____ : _____

_____ hours _____ minutes
1:30 to _____ : _____

_____ hours _____ minutes
9:00 to _____ : _____

_____ hours _____ minutes
3:00 to _____ : _____

Answers will vary. Beginning and ending times should be consistent with elapsed time.

Notes for Home Your child decided how long he or she would like to spend for an activity and wrote the ending time in digital format. *Home Activity:* Ask your child to think of one more activity he or she enjoys doing and write the beginning and ending times for it.

106 Use with pages 379–380.

Name _____

Critical Thinking

Put the pictures in the correct order.
Write 1, 2, 3, or 4.

1   4   3   2

2   3   4   1

3   2   1   4

Notes for Home Your child sequenced each row of pictures in correct order by writing the number 1, 2, 3, or 4 below each picture. *Home Activity:* Ask your child to pantomime one of the activities in the correct order.

Use with pages 383–384. **107**

Name _____

Visual Thinking

Play Tic-Tac-Time with a friend.
Try to be the first to draw times on clocks
that show the time in the correct order.
You can go from left to right, from top to bottom,
or from corner to corner.

Answers will vary.

Notes for Home Your child played a game drawing clocks that show the time in correct order. *Home Activity:* Ask your child to choose one row that was marked and figure out the time difference between the first and last clocks.

108 Use with pages 385–386.

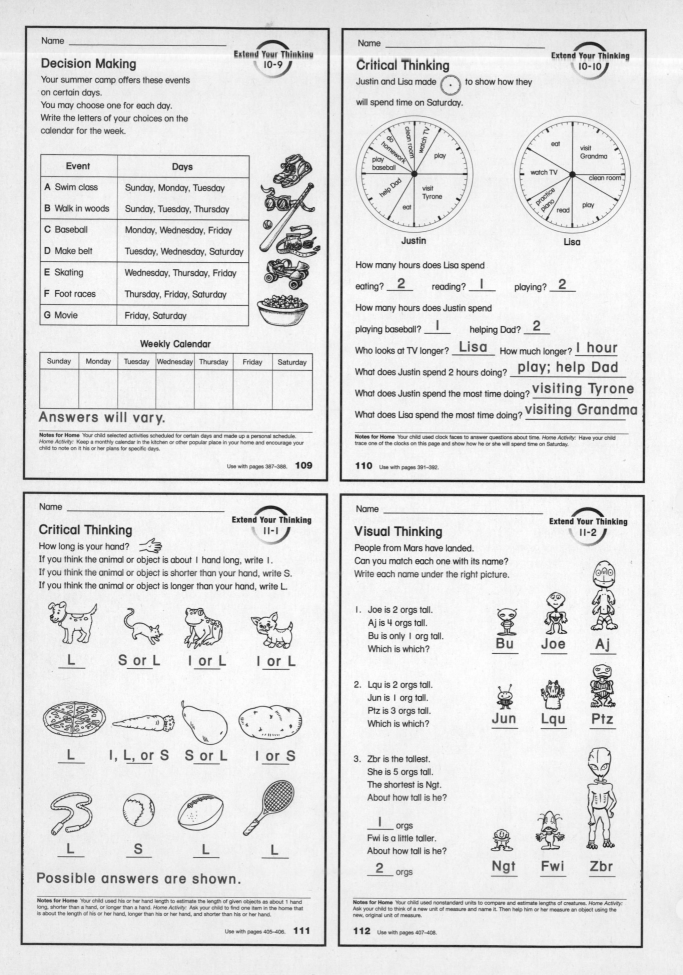

Decision Making

Your summer camp offers these events
on certain days.
You may choose one for each day.
Write the letters of your choices on the
calendar for the week.

Event	Days
A Swim class	Sunday, Monday, Tuesday
B Walk in woods	Sunday, Tuesday, Thursday
C Baseball	Monday, Wednesday, Friday
D Make belt	Tuesday, Wednesday, Saturday
E Skating	Wednesday, Thursday, Friday
F Foot races	Thursday, Friday, Saturday
G Movie	Friday, Saturday

Weekly Calendar

Sunday	Monday	Tuesday	Wednesday	Thursday	Friday	Saturday

Answers will vary.

Notes for Home Your child selected activities scheduled for certain days and made up a personal schedule. *Home Activity:* Keep a monthly calendar in the kitchen or other popular place in your home and encourage your child to note on it his or her plans for specific days.

Use with pages 387–388. **109**

Critical Thinking

Justin and Lisa made ⊙ to show how they
will spend time on Saturday.

Justin

Lisa

How many hours does Lisa spend

eating? __2__ reading? __1__ playing? __2__

How many hours does Justin spend

playing baseball? __1__ helping Dad? __2__

Who looks at TV longer? __Lisa__ How much longer? __1 hour__

What does Justin spend 2 hours doing? __play; help Dad__

What does Justin spend the most time doing? __visiting Tyrone__

What does Lisa spend the most time doing? __visiting Grandma__

Notes for Home Your child used clock faces to answer questions about time. *Home Activity:* Have your child trace one of the clocks on this page and show how he or she will spend time on Saturday.

110 Use with pages 391–392.

Critical Thinking

How long is your hand?
If you think the animal or object is about 1 hand long, write 1.
If you think the animal or object is shorter than your hand, write S.
If you think the animal or object is longer than your hand, write L.

__L__   __S or L__   __1 or L__   __1 or L__

__L__   __1, L, or S__   __S or L__   __1 or S__

__L__   __S__   __L__   __L__

Possible answers are shown.

Notes for Home Your child used his or her hand length to estimate the length of given objects as about 1 hand long, shorter than a hand, or longer than a hand. *Home Activity:* Ask your child to find one item in the home that is about the length of his or her hand, longer than his or her hand, and shorter than his or her hand.

Use with pages 405–406. **111**

Visual Thinking

People from Mars have landed.
Can you match each one with its name?
Write each name under the right picture.

1. Joe is 2 orgs tall.
   Aj is 4 orgs tall.
   Bu is only 1 org tall.
   Which is which?

   Bu   **Joe**   **Aj**

2. Lqu is 2 orgs tall.
   Jun is 1 org tall.
   Ptz is 3 orgs tall.
   Which is which?

   Jun   **Lqu**   **Ptz**

3. Zbr is the tallest.
   She is 5 orgs tall.
   The shortest is Ngt.
   About how tall is he?

   __1__ orgs
   Fwi is a little taller.
   About how tall is he?

   __2__ orgs

   Ngt   **Fwi**   **Zbr**

Notes for Home Your child used nonstandard units to compare and estimate lengths of creatures. *Home Activity:* Ask your child to think of a new unit of measure and name it. Then help him or her measure an object using the new, original unit of measure.

112 Use with pages 407–408.

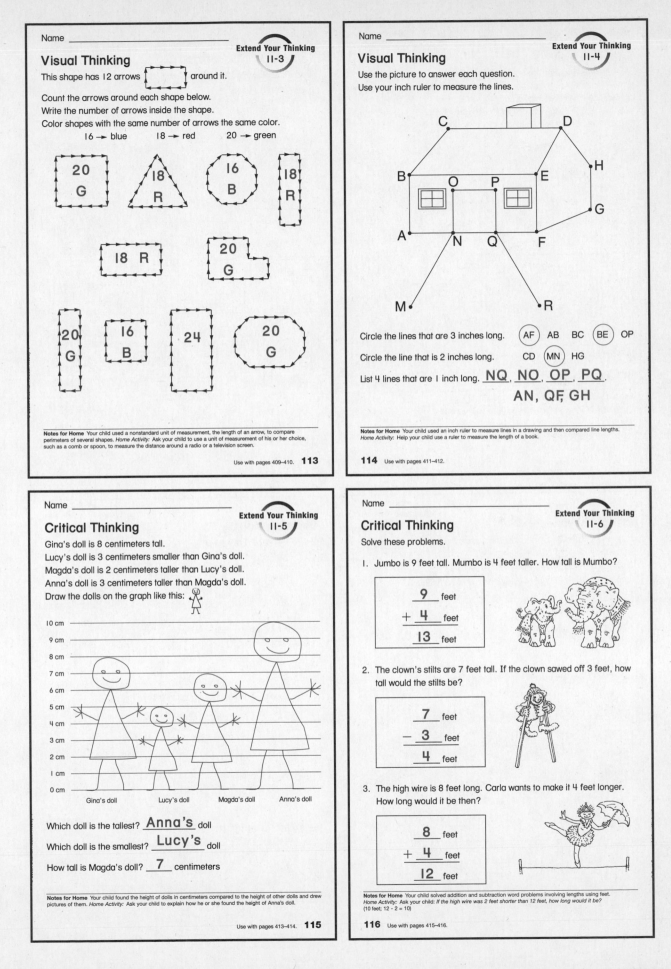

Visual Thinking

This shape has 12 arrows around it.

Count the arrows around each shape below.
Write the number of arrows inside the shape.
Color shapes with the same number of arrows the same color.

16 → blue   18 → red   20 → green

20 G

18 R

16 B

18 R

18 R

20 G

20 G

16 B

24

20 G

Visual Thinking

Use the picture to answer each question.
Use your inch ruler to measure the lines.

Circle the lines that are 3 inches long.   (AF) AB BC (BE) OP

Circle the line that is 2 inches long.   CD (MN) HG

List 4 lines that are 1 inch long. __NQ__, __NO__, __OP__, __PQ__.
__AN__, __QF__, __GH__

Critical Thinking

Gina's doll is 8 centimeters tall.
Lucy's doll is 3 centimeters smaller than Gina's doll.
Magda's doll is 2 centimeters taller than Lucy's doll.
Anna's doll is 3 centimeters taller than Magda's doll.
Draw the dolls on the graph like this:

10 cm	
9 cm	
8 cm	
7 cm	
6 cm	
5 cm	
4 cm	
3 cm	
2 cm	
1 cm	
0 cm	

Gina's doll   Lucy's doll   Magda's doll   Anna's doll

Which doll is the tallest? __Anna's__ doll

Which doll is the smallest? __Lucy's__ doll

How tall is Magda's doll? __7__ centimeters

Critical Thinking

Solve these problems.

1. Jumbo is 9 feet tall. Mumbo is 4 feet taller. How tall is Mumbo?

$$\begin{array}{r} 9 \text{ feet} \\ + 4 \text{ feet} \\ \hline 13 \text{ feet} \end{array}$$

2. The clown's stilts are 7 feet tall. If the clown sawed off 3 feet, how tall would the stilts be?

$$\begin{array}{r} 7 \text{ feet} \\ - 3 \text{ feet} \\ \hline 4 \text{ feet} \end{array}$$

3. The high wire is 8 feet long. Carla wants to make it 4 feet longer. How long would it be then?

$$\begin{array}{r} 8 \text{ feet} \\ + 4 \text{ feet} \\ \hline 12 \text{ feet} \end{array}$$

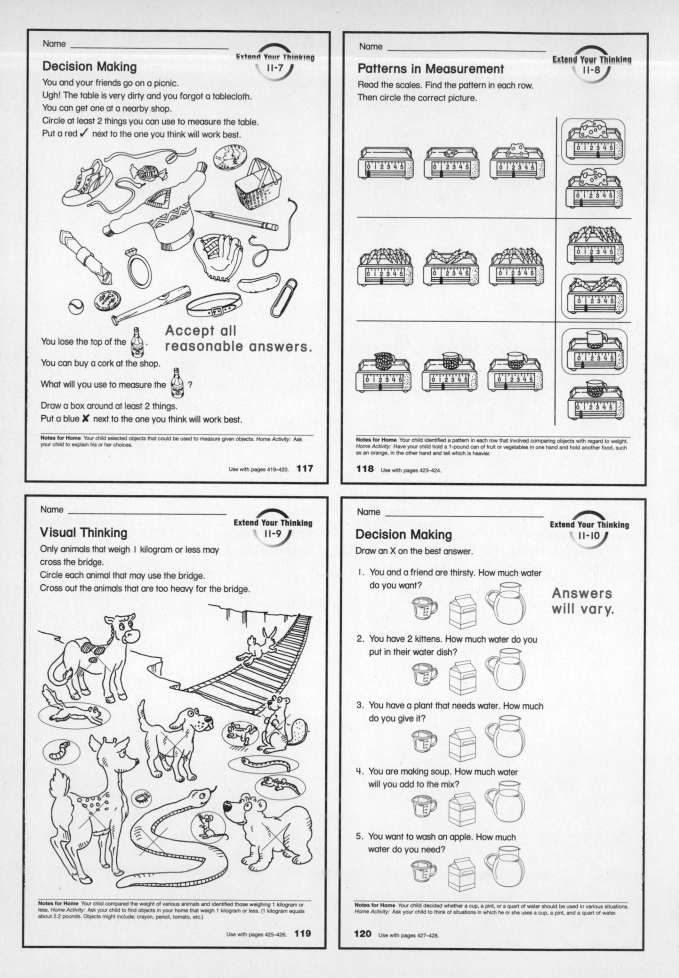

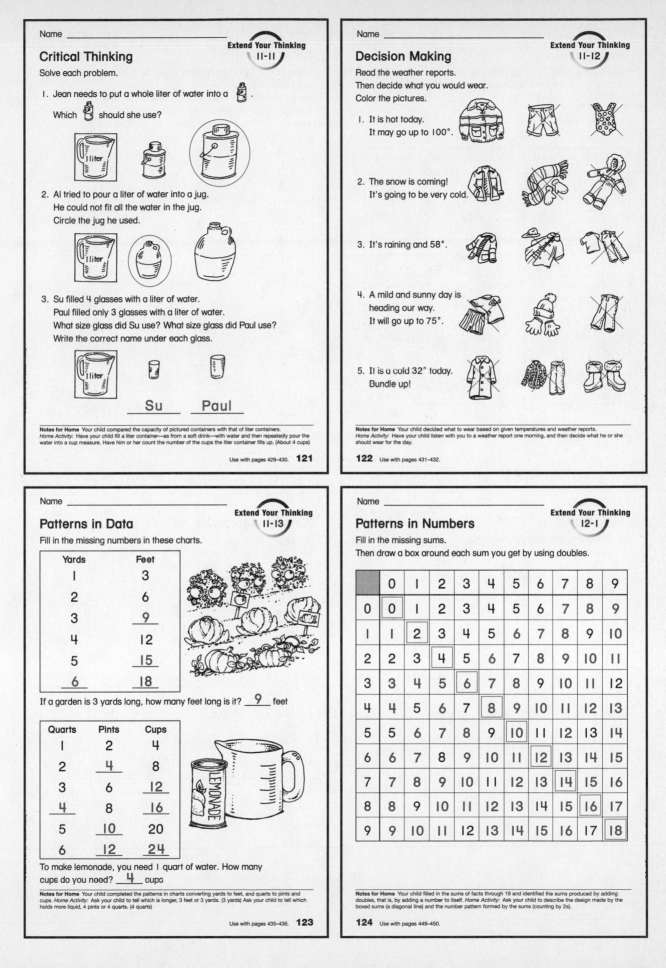

Name _____

Critical Thinking

Solve each problem.

1. Jean needs to put a whole liter of water into a ⬚.

   Which ⬚ should she use?

2. Al tried to pour a liter of water into a jug.
   He could not fit all the water in the jug.
   Circle the jug he used.

3. Su filled 4 glasses with a liter of water.
   Paul filled only 3 glasses with a liter of water.
   What size glass did Su use? What size glass did Paul use?
   Write the correct name under each glass.

   Su   Paul

Notes for Home Your child compared the capacity of pictured containers with that of liter containers.
Home Activity: Have your child fill a liter container—as from a soft drink—with water and then repeatedly pour the
water into a cup measure. Have him or her count the number of the cups the liter container fills up. (About 4 cups)

Use with pages 429–430. **121**

Name _____

Decision Making

Read the weather reports.
Then decide what you would wear.
Color the pictures.

1. It is hot today.
   It may go up to 100°.

2. The snow is coming!
   It's going to be very cold.

3. It's raining and 58°.

4. A mild and sunny day is
   heading our way.
   It will go up to 75°.

5. It is a cold 32° today.
   Bundle up!

Notes for Home Your child decided what to wear based on given temperatures and weather reports.
Home Activity: Have your child listen with you to a weather report one morning, and then decide what he or she
should wear for the day.

122 Use with pages 431–432.

Name _____

Patterns in Data

Fill in the missing numbers in these charts.

Yards	Feet
1	3
2	6
3	9
4	12
5	15
6	18

If a garden is 3 yards long, how many feet long is it? _9_ feet

Quarts	Pints	Cups
1	2	4
2	4	8
3	6	12
4	8	16
5	10	20
6	12	24

To make lemonade, you need 1 quart of water. How many
cups do you need? _4_ cups

Notes for Home Your child completed the patterns in charts converting yards to feet, and quarts to pints and
cups. *Home Activity:* Ask your child to tell which is longer, 3 feet or 3 yards. (3 yards) Ask your child to tell which
holds more liquid, 4 pints or 4 quarts. (4 quarts)

Use with pages 435–436. **123**

Name _____

Patterns in Numbers

Fill in the missing sums.
Then draw a box around each sum you get by using doubles.

	0	1	2	3	4	5	6	7	8	9
0	0	1	2	3	4	5	6	7	8	9
1	1	2	3	4	5	6	7	8	9	10
2	2	3	4	5	6	7	8	9	10	11
3	3	4	5	6	7	8	9	10	11	12
4	4	5	6	7	8	9	10	11	12	13
5	5	6	7	8	9	10	11	12	13	14
6	6	7	8	9	10	11	12	13	14	15
7	7	8	9	10	11	12	13	14	15	16
8	8	9	10	11	12	13	14	15	16	17
9	9	10	11	12	13	14	15	16	17	18

Notes for Home Your child filled in the sums of facts through 18 and identified the sums produced by adding
doubles, that is, by adding a number to itself. *Home Activity:* Ask your child to describe the design made by the
boxed sums (a diagonal line) and the number pattern formed by the sums (counting by 2s).

124 Use with pages 449–450.

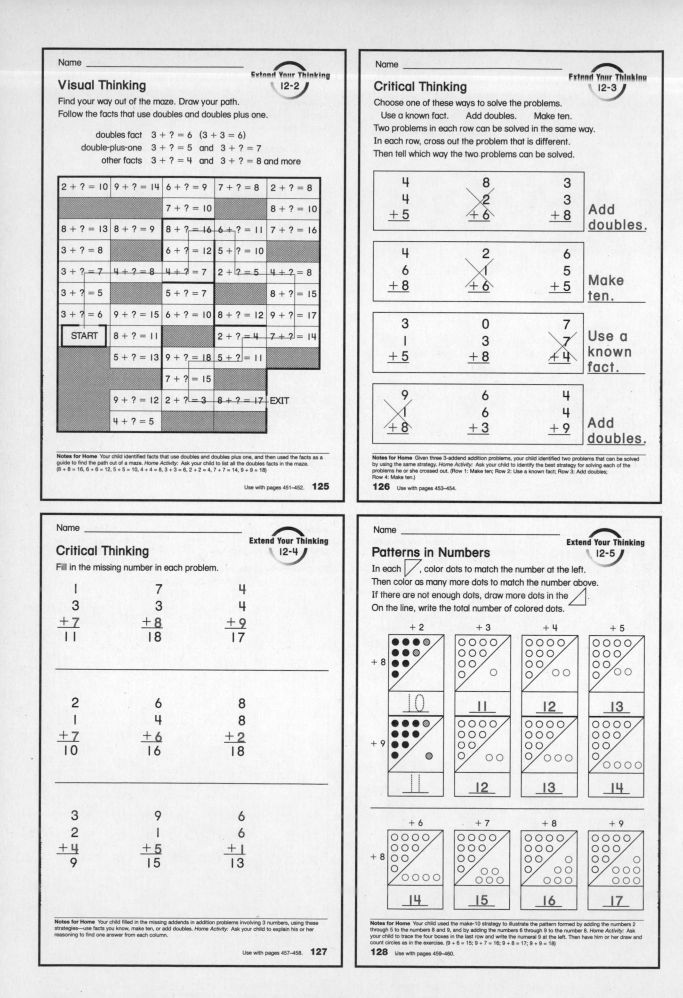

Visual Thinking

Find your way out of the maze. Draw your path.
Follow the facts that use doubles and doubles plus one.

doubles fact   3 + ? = 6   (3 + 3 = 6)
double-plus-one   3 + ? = 5 and 3 + ? = 7
other facts   3 + ? = 4 and 3 + ? = 8 and more

2 + ? = 10	9 + ? = 14	6 + ? = 9	7 + ? = 8	2 + ? = 8
	7 + ? = 10			8 + ? = 10
8 + ? = 13	8 + ? = 9	8 + ? = 16	6 + ? = 11	7 + ? = 16
3 + ? = 8		6 + ? = 12	5 + ? = 10	
3 + ? = 7	4 + ? = 8	4 + ? = 7	2 + ? = 5	4 + ? = 8
3 + ? = 5		5 + ? = 7		8 + ? = 15
3 + ? = 6	9 + ? = 15	6 + ? = 10	8 + ? = 12	9 + ? = 17
START	8 + ? = 11		2 + ? = 4	7 + ? = 14
	5 + ? = 13	9 + ? = 18	5 + ? = 11	
		7 + ? = 15		
	9 + ? = 12	2 + ? = 3	8 + ? = 17	EXIT
	4 + ? = 5			

Notes for Home Your child identified facts that use doubles and doubles plus one, and then used the facts as a guide to find the path out of a maze. *Home Activity:* Ask your child to list all the doubles facts in the maze. (8 + 8 = 16, 6 + 6 = 12, 5 + 5 = 10, 4 + 4 = 8, 3 + 3 = 6, 2 + 2 = 4, 7 + 7 = 14, 9 + 9 = 18)

Critical Thinking

Choose one of these ways to solve the problems.
  Use a known fact.   Add doubles.   Make ten.
Two problems in each row can be solved in the same way.
In each row, cross out the problem that is different.
Then tell which way the two problems can be solved.

4 4 +5	8 2̶ +6	3 3 +8	Add doubles.
4 6 +8	2̶ 1̶ +6	6 5 +5	Make ten.
3 1 +5	0 3 +8	7 7̶ +4	Use a known fact.
9̶ 1̶ +8	6 6 +3	4 4 +9	Add doubles.

Notes for Home Given three 3-addend addition problems, your child identified two problems that can be solved by using the same strategy. *Home Activity:* Ask your child to identify the best strategy for solving each of the problems he or she crossed out. (Row 1: Make ten; Row 2: Use a known fact; Row 3: Add doubles; Row 4: Make ten.)

Critical Thinking

Fill in the missing number in each problem.

1 3 +7 11	7 3 +8 18	4 4 +9 17
2 1 +7 10	6 4 +6 16	8 8 +2 18
3 2 +4 9	9 1 +5 15	6 6 +1 13

Notes for Home Your child filled in the missing addends in addition problems involving 3 numbers, using these strategies—use facts you know, make ten, or add doubles. *Home Activity:* Ask your child to explain his or her reasoning to find one answer from each column.

Patterns in Numbers

In each ◹, color dots to match the number at the left.
Then color as many more dots to match the number above.
If there are not enough dots, draw more dots in the ◹.
On the line, write the total number of colored dots.

Notes for Home Your child used the make-10 strategy to illustrate the pattern formed by adding the numbers 2 through 5 to the numbers 8 and 9, and by adding the numbers 6 through 9 to the number 8. *Home Activity:* Ask your child to trace the four boxes in the last row and write the numeral 9 at the left. Then have him or her draw and count circles as in the exercise. (9 + 6 = 15; 9 + 7 = 16; 9 + 8 = 17; 9 + 9 = 18)

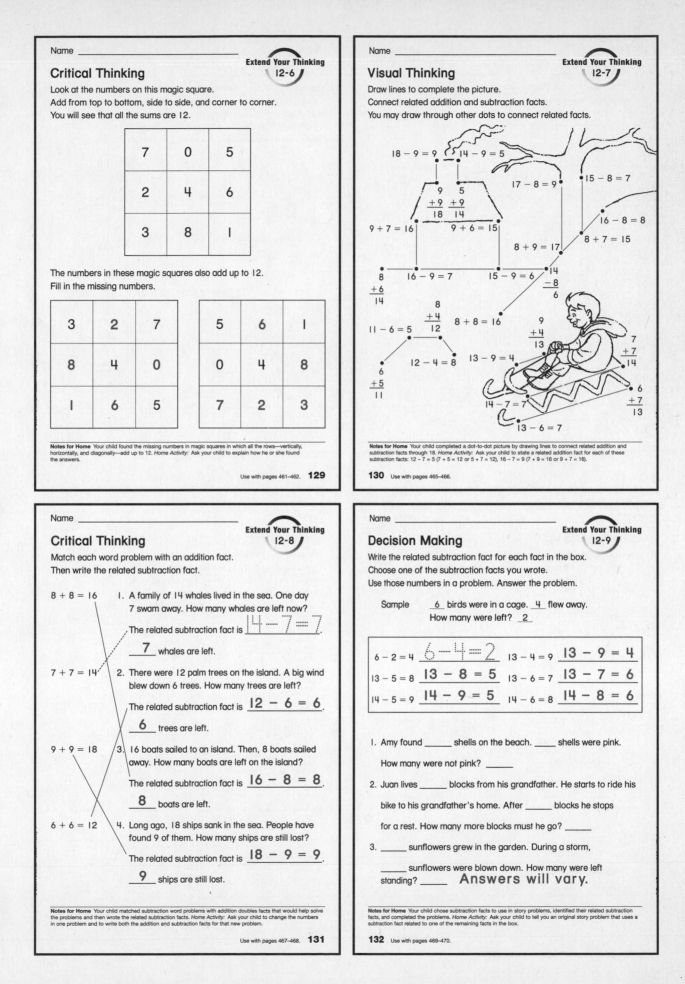

Critical Thinking

Look at the numbers on this magic square.
Add from top to bottom, side to side, and corner to corner.
You will see that all the sums are 12.

7	0	5
2	4	6
3	8	1

The numbers in these magic squares also add up to 12.
Fill in the missing numbers.

3	2	7
8	4	0
1	6	5

5	6	1
0	4	8
7	2	3

Notes for Home Your child found the missing numbers in magic squares in which all the rows—vertically, horizontally, and diagonally—add up to 12. Home Activity: Ask your child to explain how he or she found the answers.

Use with pages 461–462. **129**

Visual Thinking

Draw lines to complete the picture.
Connect related addition and subtraction facts.
You may draw through other dots to connect related facts.

$18 - 9 = 9$ $14 - 9 = 5$ $17 - 8 = 9$ $15 - 8 = 7$

9 +9 18   5 +9 14

$9 + 7 = 16$ $9 + 6 = 15$ $16 - 8 = 8$

$8 + 9 = 17$ $8 + 7 = 15$

8 +6 14 $16 - 9 = 7$ $15 - 9 = 6$ 14 -8 6

8 +4 12 $8 + 8 = 16$ 9 +4 13

$11 - 6 = 5$

6 +5 11 $12 - 4 = 8$ $13 - 9 = 4$ 7 +7 14

   $14 - 7 = 7$ 6 +7 13

$13 - 6 = 7$

Notes for Home Your child completed a dot-to-dot picture by drawing lines to connect related addition and subtraction facts through 18. Home Activity: Ask your child to state a related addition fact for each of these subtraction facts: 12 − 7 = 5 (7 + 5 = 12 or 5 + 7 = 12), 16 − 9 = 7 (7 + 9 = 16 or 9 + 7 = 16).

130 Use with pages 465–466.

Critical Thinking

Match each word problem with an addition fact.
Then write the related subtraction fact.

$8 + 8 = 16$

$7 + 7 = 14$

$9 + 9 = 18$

$6 + 6 = 12$

1. A family of 14 whales lived in the sea. One day 7 swam away. How many whales are left now?

The related subtraction fact is $14 - 7 = 7$.

___7___ whales are left.

2. There were 12 palm trees on the island. A big wind blew down 6 trees. How many trees are left?

The related subtraction fact is $12 - 6 = 6$.

___6___ trees are left.

3. 16 boats sailed to an island. Then, 8 boats sailed away. How many boats are left on the island?

The related subtraction fact is $16 - 8 = 8$.

___8___ boats are left.

4. Long ago, 18 ships sank in the sea. People have found 9 of them. How many ships are still lost?

The related subtraction fact is $18 - 9 = 9$.

___9___ ships are still lost.

Notes for Home Your child matched subtraction word problems with addition doubles facts that would help solve the problems and then wrote the related subtraction facts. Home Activity: Ask your child to change the numbers in one problem and to write both the addition and subtraction facts for that new problem.

Use with pages 467–468. **131**

Decision Making

Write the related subtraction fact for each fact in the box.
Choose one of the subtraction facts you wrote.
Use those numbers in a problem. Answer the problem.

Sample ___6___ birds were in a cage. ___4___ flew away.
How many were left? ___2___

$6 - 2 = 4$ $6 - 4 = 2$	$13 - 4 = 9$ $13 - 9 = 4$
$13 - 5 = 8$ $13 - 8 = 5$	$13 - 6 = 7$ $13 - 7 = 6$
$14 - 5 = 9$ $14 - 9 = 5$	$14 - 6 = 8$ $14 - 8 = 6$

1. Amy found _____ shells on the beach. _____ shells were pink.

How many were not pink? _____

2. Juan lives _____ blocks from his grandfather. He starts to ride his

bike to his grandfather's home. After _____ blocks he stops

for a rest. How many more blocks must he go? _____

3. _____ sunflowers grew in the garden. During a storm,

_____ sunflowers were blown down. How many were left
standing? _____ **Answers will vary.**

Notes for Home Your child chose subtraction facts to use in story problems, identified their related subtraction facts, and completed the problems. Home Activity: Ask your child to tell you an original story problem that uses a subtraction fact related to one of the remaining facts in the box.

132 Use with pages 469–470.

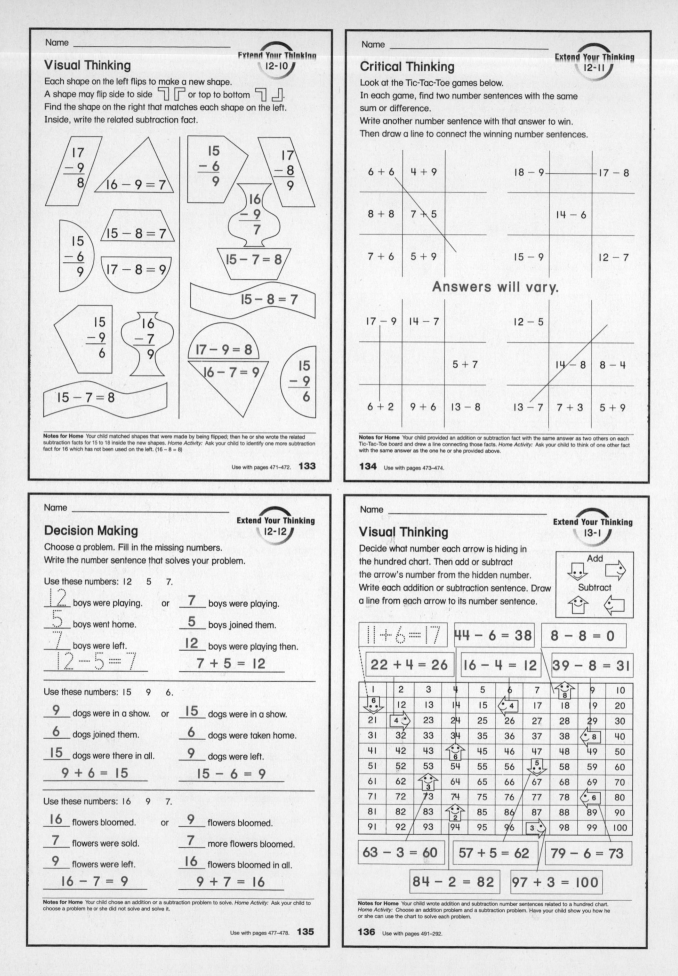

Visual Thinking

Each shape on the left flips to make a new shape.
A shape may flip side to side ⌐⌐ or top to bottom ⌐⌐.
Find the shape on the right that matches each shape on the left.
Inside, write the related subtraction fact.

17
− 9
8

16 − 9 = 7

15
− 6
9

17
− 8
9

16
− 9
7

15
− 6
9

15 − 8 = 7

17 − 8 = 9

15 − 7 = 8

15 − 8 = 7

15
− 9
6

16
− 7
9

17 − 9 = 8

16 − 7 = 9

15
− 9
6

15 − 7 = 8

Notes for Home Your child matched shapes that were made by being flipped; then he or she wrote the related subtraction facts for 15 to 18 inside the new shapes. Home Activity: Ask your child to identify one more subtraction fact for 16 which has not been used on the left. (16 − 8 = 8)

Use with pages 471–472. **133**

Critical Thinking

Look at the Tic-Tac-Toe games below.
In each game, find two number sentences with the same
sum or difference.
Write another number sentence with that answer to win.
Then draw a line to connect the winning number sentences.

6 + 6	4 + 9
8 + 8	7 + 5
7 + 6	5 + 9

18 − 9	17 − 8
	14 − 6
15 − 9	12 − 7

Answers will vary.

17 − 9	14 − 7
	5 + 7
6 + 2	9 + 6	13 − 8

12 − 5	
14 − 8	8 − 4
13 − 7	7 + 3	5 + 9

Notes for Home Your child provided an addition or subtraction fact with the same answer as two others on each Tic-Tac-Toe board and drew a line connecting those facts. Home Activity: Ask your child to think of one other fact with the same answer as the one he or she provided above.

134 Use with pages 473–474.

Decision Making

Choose a problem. Fill in the missing numbers.
Write the number sentence that solves your problem.

Use these numbers: 12   5   7.

12 boys were playing.   or   7 boys were playing.
5 boys went home.   5 boys joined them.
7 boys were left.   12 boys were playing then.
12 − 5 = 7   7 + 5 = 12

Use these numbers: 15   9   6.

9 dogs were in a show.   or   15 dogs were in a show.
6 dogs joined them.   6 dogs were taken home.
15 dogs were there in all.   9 dogs were left.
9 + 6 = 15   15 − 6 = 9

Use these numbers: 16   9   7.

16 flowers bloomed.   or   9 flowers bloomed.
7 flowers were sold.   7 more flowers bloomed.
9 flowers were left.   16 flowers bloomed in all.
16 − 7 = 9   9 + 7 = 16

Notes for Home Your child chose an addition or a subtraction problem to solve. Home Activity: Ask your child to choose a problem he or she did not solve and solve it.

Use with pages 477–478. **135**

Visual Thinking

Decide what number each arrow is hiding in
the hundred chart. Then add or subtract
the arrow's number from the hidden number.
Write each addition or subtraction sentence. Draw
a line from each arrow to its number sentence.

Add
Subtract

| 11 + 6 = 17 | 44 − 6 = 38 | 8 − 8 = 0 |
| 22 + 4 = 26 | 16 − 4 = 12 | 39 − 8 = 31 |

1	2	3	4	5	6	7	8	9	10
6	12	13	14	15	4	17	18	19	20
21	4	23	24	25	26	27	28	29	30
31	32	33	34	35	36	37	38	8	40
41	42	43	6	45	46	47	48	49	50
51	52	53	54	55	56	5	58	59	60
61	62	3	64	65	66	67	68	69	70
71	72	73	74	75	76	77	78	6	80
81	82	83	2	85	86	87	88	89	90
91	92	93	94	95	96	3	98	99	100

| 63 − 3 = 60 | 57 + 5 = 62 | 79 − 6 = 73 |

| 84 − 2 = 82 | 97 + 3 = 100 |

Notes for Home Your child wrote addition and subtraction number sentences related to a hundred chart. Home Activity: Choose an addition problem and a subtraction problem. Have your child show you how he or she can use the chart to solve each problem.

136 Use with pages 491–292.

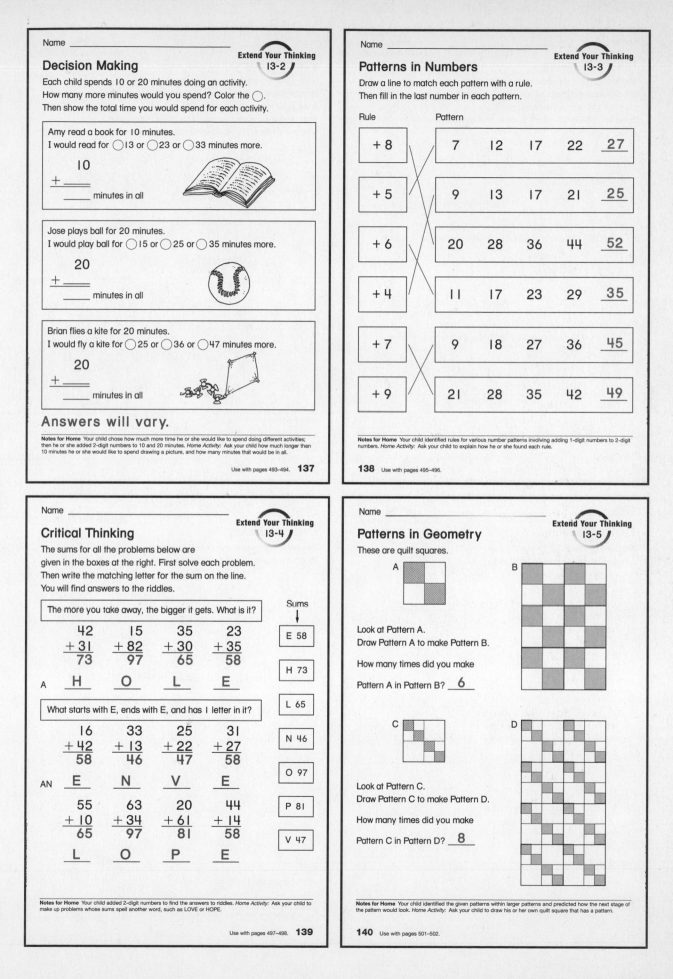

Decision Making

Each child spends 10 or 20 minutes doing an activity.
How many more minutes would you spend? Color the ◯.
Then show the total time you would spend for each activity.

Amy read a book for 10 minutes.
I would read for ◯13 or ◯23 or ◯33 minutes more.

10
+ _____
_____ minutes in all

Jose plays ball for 20 minutes.
I would play ball for ◯15 or ◯25 or ◯35 minutes more.

20
+ _____
_____ minutes in all

Brian flies a kite for 20 minutes.
I would fly a kite for ◯25 or ◯36 or ◯47 minutes more.

20
+ _____
_____ minutes in all

Answers will vary.

Notes for Home Your child chose how much more time he or she would like to spend doing different activities; then he or she added 2-digit numbers to 10 and 20 minutes. *Home Activity:* Ask your child how much longer than 10 minutes he or she would like to spend drawing a picture, and how many minutes that would be in all.

Use with pages 493–494. **137**

Patterns in Numbers

Draw a line to match each pattern with a rule.
Then fill in the last number in each pattern.

Rule	Pattern
+ 8	7 12 17 22 _27_
+ 5	9 13 17 21 _25_
+ 6	20 28 36 44 _52_
+ 4	11 17 23 29 _35_
+ 7	9 18 27 36 _45_
+ 9	21 28 35 42 _49_

Notes for Home Your child identified rules for various number patterns involving adding 1-digit numbers to 2-digit numbers. *Home Activity:* Ask your child to explain how he or she found each rule.

138 Use with pages 495–496.

Critical Thinking

The sums for all the problems below are
given in the boxes at the right. First solve each problem.
Then write the matching letter for the sum on the line.
You will find answers to the riddles.

The more you take away, the bigger it gets. What is it?

42	15	35	23
+ 31	+ 82	+ 30	+ 35
73	97	65	58

A H   O   L   E

What starts with E, ends with E, and has 1 letter in it?

16	33	25	31
+ 42	+ 13	+ 22	+ 27
58	46	47	58

AN E   N   V   E

55	63	20	44
+ 10	+ 34	+ 61	+ 14
65	97	81	58

L   O   P   E

Sums
↓

E 58

H 73

L 65

N 46

O 97

P 81

V 47

Notes for Home Your child added 2-digit numbers to find the answers to riddles. *Home Activity:* Ask your child to make up problems whose sums spell another word, such as LOVE or HOPE.

Use with pages 497–498. **139**

Patterns in Geometry

These are quilt squares.

A

B

Look at Pattern A.
Draw Pattern A to make Pattern B.

How many times did you make

Pattern A in Pattern B? _6_

C

D

Look at Pattern C.
Draw Pattern C to make Pattern D.

How many times did you make

Pattern C in Pattern D? _8_

Notes for Home Your child identified the given patterns within larger patterns and predicted how the next stage of the pattern would look. *Home Activity:* Ask your child to draw his or her own quilt square that has a pattern.

140 Use with pages 501–502.

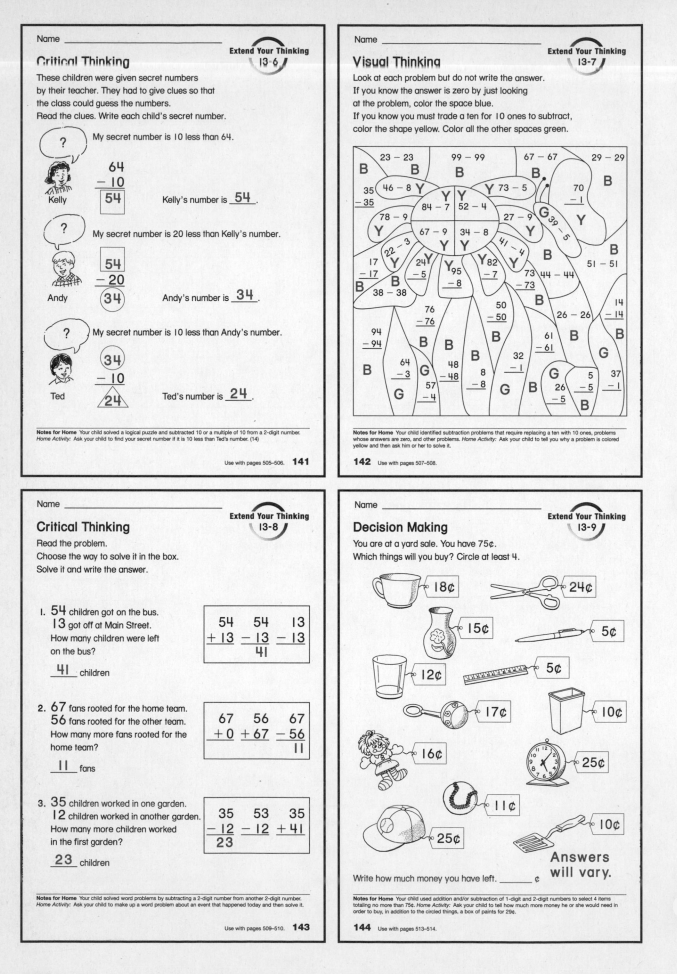

Critical Thinking

These children were given secret numbers by their teacher. They had to give clues so that the class could guess the numbers.
Read the clues. Write each child's secret number.

? My secret number is 10 less than 64.

Kelly
$$\begin{array}{r} 64 \\ -10 \\ \hline 54 \end{array}$$

Kelly's number is __54__.

? My secret number is 20 less than Kelly's number.

Andy
$$\begin{array}{r} 54 \\ -20 \\ \hline 34 \end{array}$$

Andy's number is __34__.

? My secret number is 10 less than Andy's number.

Ted
$$\begin{array}{r} 34 \\ -10 \\ \hline 24 \end{array}$$

Ted's number is __24__.

Notes for Home Your child solved a logical puzzle and subtracted 10 or a multiple of 10 from a 2-digit number. *Home Activity:* Ask your child to find your secret number if it is 10 less than Ted's number. (14)

Use with pages 505–506. **141**

Visual Thinking

Look at each problem but do not write the answer.
If you know the answer is zero by just looking at the problem, color the space blue.
If you know you must trade a ten for 10 ones to subtract, color the shape yellow. Color all the other spaces green.

Notes for Home Your child identified subtraction problems that require replacing a ten with 10 ones, problems whose answers are zero, and other problems. *Home Activity:* Ask your child to tell you why a problem is colored yellow and then ask him or her to solve it.

142 Use with pages 507–508.

Critical Thinking

Read the problem.
Choose the way to solve it in the box.
Solve it and write the answer.

1. 54 children got on the bus.
   13 got off at Main Street.
   How many children were left on the bus?

   $$\begin{array}{ccc} 54 & 54 & 13 \\ +13 & -13 & -13 \\ & \overline{41} & \end{array}$$

   __41__ children

2. 67 fans rooted for the home team.
   56 fans rooted for the other team.
   How many more fans rooted for the home team?

   $$\begin{array}{ccc} 67 & 56 & 67 \\ +0 & +67 & -56 \\ & & \overline{11} \end{array}$$

   __11__ fans

3. 35 children worked in one garden.
   12 children worked in another garden.
   How many more children worked in the first garden?

   $$\begin{array}{ccc} 35 & 53 & 35 \\ -12 & -12 & +41 \\ \overline{23} & & \end{array}$$

   __23__ children

Notes for Home Your child solved word problems by subtracting a 2-digit number from another 2-digit number. *Home Activity:* Ask your child to make up a word problem about an event that happened today and then solve it.

Use with pages 509–510. **143**

Decision Making

You are at a yard sale. You have 75¢.
Which things will you buy? Circle at least 4.

18¢   24¢   15¢   5¢   12¢   5¢   17¢   10¢   16¢   25¢   11¢   25¢   10¢

Answers will vary.

Write how much money you have left. _____ ¢

Notes for Home Your child used addition and/or subtraction of 1-digit and 2-digit numbers to select 4 items totaling no more than 75¢. *Home Activity:* Ask your child to tell how much more money he or she would need in order to buy, in addition to the circled things, a box of paints for 29¢.

144 Use with pages 513–514.